A
DICTIONARY
OF
HAIKU

Jane Reichhold

A
DICTIONARY
OF
HAIKU

Second Edition
1993 - 2013

Jane Reichhold

AHA Books

A Dictionary of Haiku
Second Edition

Book and haiku Copyright © Jane Reichhold 2013.
Collages Copyright © Werner Reichhold 2013.

ISBN: 0-944676-24-3

Requests to quote haiku should be addressed to:

AHA Books
P.O. Box 767
Gualala, CA 95445

Jane@AHApoetry.com
www.AHApoetry.com
www.forum.AHApoetry.com

TABLE OF CONTENTS

questioning
remembering
sad
satisfaction
shy
sleepless
slowing down
soaring spirits
thankfulness
thoughtful
understanding
unhappy
unfaithful
unknown
worship
wishes
worry

arrival of summer
August
departing summer
dog days
Fourth of July
summer passing
summer solstice

breezes
clouds
comet
coolness
dawn
darkness
dew
drought
evening
fog
heat
light
lightning

long day
Milky Way
mist
moon
moon rise
moon set
night
rain
rainbow
sky
south wind
stars
storm
sun
sunrise
sunset
sunshine
thunder
twilight
warmth
winds

beach
canyon
caves
cliffs
creek
desert
earth
earthquake
fields
hills
island
lagoon
lakes
land
landslide
lava
meadow
mountains

Introduction
D.S. Lliteras

The scope of this work is breathtaking. It is a true reflection of a lifetime devoted to studying, writing, and fighting for haiku in English. Jane Reichhold has been a true haiku warrior who has been on the Western cultural battlefield for over five decades. Form and structure have been her weapons. The *here-and-now* has been her guide. And her uncompromising poetic presence has been her battle flag for poets to rally around for years.

Jane Reichhold is also a true believer in the need for cross cultural influences in literature — in this case between the East and the West — but more specifically, between Japan and America. And although these two cultures and languages in many ways are polar opposites, they do have one universal thing in common: their humanness. Reichhold's haiku is filled with humanness, filled with literary spirit, filled with religious spirit and, therefore, she reaches into the souls of those who want to know more about what's in the heart of things.

Concerning the essence of haiku itself: haiku tries to offer a balance between the relative and the absolute and, in so doing, causes the reader to experience the author's found *here-and-now* — hence, completing the haiku offered to them. But Reichhold believes that this essence of the *here-and-now* can also be connected to a seasonal-word, which is often ignored or avoided or simply omitted by writers of haiku in English because of the brevity of the form. To many, it takes up too much room in a form of so few syllables. And yet, she understands that the seasonal-word is literally a fundamental element of haiku that can be incorporated, if a haiku in English is to be considered a haiku at all. And so, you have before you, *A Dictionary of Haiku*, which beautifully illustrates how seasonal references are applied or implied for haiku to simply be — haiku.

In the final analysis, the question is, do we know what we are talking about when we address the poetic form of haiku in English? In other words, do we know what we are doing when we try to construct and attach rules to this art form in English? Ultimately, and metaphysically, I can't answer that. Because in the final analysis, haiku, like all high art is an enigma. Its origin is culturally specific to Japan and, yet, it has found its place in the Western world where it continuously struggles to find clearer definitions. This is the ground on which Reichhold has stood. She is a Western woman who has demanded definitions for haiku in English, in German, in Spanish, in any language of the West. This, of course, has made her a friend to some and an opponent to others.

Poetry is a hard trade, an unforgiving trade, even an ungrateful one. But Jane Reichhold has not been in this for the reward. Haiku is its own reward.

NOTES TO THE SECOND EDITION

The first edition of *A Dictionary of Haiku* was published in 1992. At the time we had printer-quality copy machine so we printed 300 copies of the 391 page book on it and collated it by walking around tables. It was professionally bound in Fort Bragg in a maroon linen paperback with gold leaf lettering.

When I discovered recently that used copies were selling for $350 I got the idea of reprinting it with a print-on-demand facility. The haiku from that edition were on the AHApoetry.com web site so I could capture them. However, the old type-setting program I had used had been taken over by Word which refused to make heads and numbering in the old way.

It seemed to me that all the work that was going into a reprint of material that was free on the web could be better spent in making a second edition of *A Dictionary of Haiku* using the haiku I had written since 1993.

There are about the same number of haiku in this book but I made some small changes in the way the poems are presented and the pages are larger. As you read you will find some haiku are not correctly placed according to the alphabet. Those are revisions. I left them so you could find them.

I always felt the New Year's section was so small it was negligible, so I decided to add much of the material that was the result of religion to fill the fifth season.

In a few cases I had written haiku sequences so I put them in their original order instead of placing the haiku alphabetically as they are in the rest of the categories.

Also, many haiku seemed to fit into several different categories so when this happened I let it be. These are not all the haiku I wrote in these twenty years. I did cull out many that would have no meaning for others or seemed not up to my standards today.

I hope you will find as much pleasure in reading and studying these haiku as I have had in living them.

Blessed be!

Jane Reichhold
April, 2013

SPRING

SPRING Moods

coping

attention to detail
attending the event
on the wrong day

hating my cast
yet the half-moon shines
on the bright side

not sharing
root nor form or gesture
just this day

safe delivery
birth's traditional music
of pain

wide beach
no room for
angry feelings

desire

caught
in her eyes
his words

first meeting
questions shove aside
the shy smile

hanging by a thread
the button on her blouse
his eyes held fast

having an affair
a daughter forgets her mother
had several

setting a trap
the noose of desire
encircles nothing

storm-tossed willows
I too wish to run
with the wind

sunset alone
even I am ready
for love

the call
of her cleavage
first notes

thin branches
I want to be taken
by someone

this my skin
for you to touch
between us

wearing his shirt
does he know he left in it
the sexy feeling?

dreaming

appearing
me in your dream
you in my. . .

moon reverie
seeing so clearly
that youthful lover

1

waiting for someone
the vacant house high
on a hill

emptiness
nothing fills
the emptiness of the question
where are they?

the empty nest
my daughter's house
after the wedding

joy
floating away
a twig dropped
from the bridge

getting lost
in apple blossoms
applause

graceless
joy in the young
charm

morning moon
the best of the night
lingers for me

my grown son
teaching me to make a graft
just like dad did

our days
drifting on beaches
dissolve into stars

pale pink and blue
the day arranges itself
under my eyelids

spring again
in the Japanese garden
Buddha's smile

spring joy
ripening grass
for August life

the breeze
while wearing his boxer shorts
all the way up

the tiniest flower
because you touched it
stains me deeply

waking up nude
moonset over the sea
our shining

love
after she passed
still wearing the smile
she gave him

a pair reunited
in their love of jazz
blues

apple dapple
bare on the grass
lovers

cupping her face
both of his hands
her perfume

first dream of love
the summer sleep
of honey suckle

flirting with boys
in the doctor's office
only toddlers

he peeks
in the rearview mirror
at her butt

holding hands
in his pocket
I'm 14 again

like your scars
known by my fingers
your name

love is blind
with her he can't see
the full moon

love songs
in the flute player's face
grief

music
in the grass
lovers

one song all night
someone in my son's room
is in love

pleasure
coin of the far country
love

sea kisses
the off-shore wind brings
your lips closer

she shuts her eyes
still he loves her
laugh

spring time
Buddha's eyes are half-closed
as he watches

teen-age love
mohair from her sweater
fuzz balls on his pants

the moon
in your eyes
the ancient light

unsaid
on her lips
yes

words not spoken
when you fall in love
the violin speaks

praise

lauds
before sunrise
our praising

praises
from the cheekbone
a smile

mysteries
dreams
the tightrope we walk
without a net

it tells you something
the wedding ceremony begins
with a march

pre-dawn
every departure this day
emerges now
silence
between objects known
others becoming

slow waiting
for the moon to set
babies to be born

newness
a boat that sails
through generations
her belly

high speed internet
with just one click
they fall in love

first date
the pants and shirt
don't match

land's end
the adventure begins
at take-off
my friends

faces aglow with music
meeting them anew

spring again
forgetting that beet seeds
look like that

inexperienced
the t-shirt's sleeves
go up and down

new girlfriends
my grandson searches for one
in a lingerie catalog

togetherness
curled together
as if friends
turds in a toilet

you
my grandmother
as a young girl

unhappiness
among fallen petals
a tissue with lipstick traces
another story

a quarter moon
wearing this white cast
I'm not worth 2 cents

a triangle
of village love and lust
a couple splits

blue ink
a letter not written
in the iris

Mother
she finds an aphid to squash
in my garden flowers

giving to mom
all the daisies from my garden
where did you steal them flowers

good-byes
lighting the parking lot
dim flashlights

noticing my polished nails
his eyes seem to say
I think you have a lover

primrose path
I never noticed
where I was going

sitting next to me
in the empty seat
my anxiety

SPRING Occasions

beginning of spring
April arrives
among dancers tossing flowers
the village mad man

awakened from a nap
what, what the old man asks
is it spring yet

first sign of spring
ice releases the water
in the pond

Mardi Gras
after this spring
must come

spring's coming
the delivery man brings
a new mattress

birth
birth of a girl
the sea is ruffled
with small waves

lady rain
and then the cry
of the girl child

pink and blue
the day prepares
for its own birth

conception
a meeting
on the ancient path
conception

departing spring
departing spring
to remember the words
I hum the tune

Easter
Easter
I dust the poinsettia
that refuses to die

empty
yet in the Easter basket
the chocolate smell

tying ears
on the white cat
Easter morning

Father's Day
Father's Day
again the dream I'm married
to him

Father's Day
his wife's gift
a maternity tie

Flag Day
a flag waving
on the street where you live
my heart

flag day
the picnic steaks red
as his shoulders

flag day
in our remote area
there are more iris

Graduation

a June moon
the grads' party
in a new light

graduation
proud parents first video
kindergarten

June

June
a welcomed visitor
to this latitude

naming its days
graduation, vacation wedding
June

stretching out
in a patch of sunlight
June

May

a carp kite
the childless couple borrows
a big one

bright May day
the forbidden desire
to do it

May
yes you may be
a little naughty

quiet May day
teaching the birds
how to sing

Memorial Day

Memorial Day
even when bungled
taps makes me cry

Memorial Day
thinking of the people I have
put under ground

Memorial Day
the shaking flowers
on the graves

Memorial Day
the wind taking flowers
from the graves

Memorial Day
unable to remember
the wave of panic

Memorial Day
wild flowers overpower
the flags

Memorial Day
still able to remember
the shape of a wave

Mother's Day

a dozen roses
one for each grandchild
on Mother's Day

earthquake
the deep groan
of a mother

Mother's Day
a child shares with me
cinnamon candies

Mother's Day
deciding the cat
must be spayed

Mother's Day
looking at old photos
no longer alone

Mother's Day
my homemade gifts are
my three kids

Mother's Day
the house is changed
by a new baby
for Abby

Mother's Day
time to buy a gift
for myself

Mother's Day
with the hawks gone north
nest-building begins

sleeping late
on Mother's Day
the shrill phone

unable to speak
her Mother's Day greeting
into the machine

St. Patrick's Day
St. Patrick's Day
a Japanese friend introduces
green tea

weddings
blue ink
marking on the calendar
the day we wed

calling the ancestors
the wedding ceremony begins
with grandparents

honeymoon
forgetting where we parked
the car

light and shadow
married in the mountains
shining curves

marriage in heaven
to the tops of trees
come clouds

out-door wedding
the best man loans his coat
to the bride

picking polish
from her red nails
always a bridesmaid

the marriage
of wind and sea
waves

wedding bells
the clang of gifts shifting
on the curvy road

worm juice
woven in the rich girl's
silk gown

SPRING Celestial

clouds

bridging
heaven
clouds

cloud boats
sailing over the hills
spring is coming

cloud houses
peaking over the hills
spring is coming

clouds
flooding the river
with spring

clouds and earth
spinning from the sun
a warm-colored sky

clouds
the plants spring up
in sky fields

cloudy day
spindrift leaves the sea
for us

heavy rain
the ocean depths
cloud-high

inland clouds
the tops of big waves
in blue sky

stained
by not-dropped rain
a sea of clouds

world building
every rain cloud
leaves its mark

dawn

coming at dawn
my friends for a day
sea colors

dawn
fog blankets
the hills

dawn light
from the moon
a golden glow

dawn light
the world reassembled
almost new

dawn moon
with the verse written
something goes

dawn
the stars still humming
jazz riffs

glowing clouds
the not-seen moon
becomes dawn

morning light
each thing remembers
its place

morning moon
the brightness of dawn
nearly round

nearing dawn
the coming down light
from Venus

petal soft
the white pink of ideas
before dawn

rosy dawn
colors the moon
into the sea

silver water
the canoe slowed
by dawn's hush

spring dawn
darkness flies from the trees
with the bird

the sound of waves
on your sleeping face
dawn light

with a sneeze
topping the hill
sunrise

dusk
get well visitor
waiting for me at dusk
the waxing moon

fog
fog
as islands of smoke
from the south

haze
mist
over the mountain pass
a bridge

mists of May
covering the hillside
tiny white flowers

misty rain
and the plum tree
bloom as one

spring haze
at the flute's sound
cat hair

lightning
counting the miles
between the lightning
and my ear

moon
a little flat
the sea is touched
by the moon

as if new
the perfect moon
comes to earth

for the season
the moon gives its life
to the whole earth

full moon
no other ship sails
on the sea

glowing clouds
the not-seen moon
becomes dawn

half and tilted
the day moon inclines
toward the bud

in the dawn sky
the sliver of a white boat
an old moon

more paper
the biggest moon of the year
nears the horizon

morning light
comes earlier now
the clear full moon

turning to gold
the unmined moon
comes to earth

with the moon
night too disappears
into the ocean

moonlight
a soft spot
where the baby's skull opens
moonlight

moon rise
setting at dawn
the moon will rise
full tonight

moon set
moonset
I turn around to see
the sun

moonset
the sea turns pink
with dawn

morning hush
the moon sets
in a mist

morning rush
the moon sets
in a hurry

still up at dawn
the moon leaves as
blush-pink

rain
a woman dreams
a soft diamond song
rain drops

cloudy skies
so full of April
it rains again

daylong rain
a blaze of sun through clouds
and shutters

falling
the amount of rain
in a haiku

heavenly
the soft ring of rain
becomes the view

in the roar
of the mountain stream
continuous rain

misty rain
a budding branch shimmers
with all the colors

morning light
lasting all day
the rain

rain
coming to the wakeful
sleep sounds

rain drops
in a puddle crowns
of light jewels

spring rain
fallen blossoms paint
my face

spring rain
her last no
lace

spring rain
the shine on bleached grass
weighs it down

the phone rings
without answering
it begins to rain

wearing weather
everyone mentions
it's wet

rainbow

far below
the rainbow held up
by nothing at all

running down a path
the rainbow always faster
to slip over the cliff

sky

first light
the earth separates
from the sky

fog
disappearing into the sky
morning

sky spaces
between what you are
music

spring sky
fills snow-melt puddles
to its rim

stars

headlights
curved out over the sea
Venus

sun
from another planet
the glow in green grass
spring sunshine

opening a slit
between clouds and sea
the rising sun

radiance
on the edge of water
one's own center

wet sunlight
a path of worms
right to a robin

sun rise
sun rise
a warm glow covers
the setting moon

sun rise
giving me a new name
and a shadow

sun rise
the silver moon turns
to gold

wind
a breeze
bumping blossoms
bees

blowing away
end of an afternoon
the music

playing with her
and her scarf
spring winds

spring winds
a ripple in the welcome mat
comes in the door

trees and grasses bend
in such a wind the gulls
hang motionless

weaver winds
the white world of waves
spinning

wind
whipping the jump rope
fudge fudge tell the judge

SPRING Terrestrial

beach
on the beach
old eggs of the sea
rocks

suiseki
on the dry sand
roar of the sea

canyon
spring run-off
the thunder in the canyon
comes from the sky

cliffs
cliff run-off
leaping into the sky
falls

no trespassing
yet to the dangerous cliffs
spring comes

rain-soaked cliff
the trickling down is all
there is of it

earthquake
if we ask
was that an earthquake
it was very little

fields
a fallow field
moonlight comes first
to newly turned earth

thawed fields
the spring harvest
stone crop

tractors dragging
red dust on the horizon
spring fields

flood
drinking in the flood
a beer bottle in the ditch
overflows

spring flood
the slicked back grass points
the water way

flood lines
on the willows
grass stems

hills
afternoon hills
east of the sea cliff
tall clouds

eastern hills
driving into the dawn
a rosy glow

spring floods
the hill is lower
by a river

spring rain
the hills newly dyed
greengreengreen

meadows
meadow network
strung from tree to tree
birdsong

mountains
flowing into the sea
water leftover from creating
pine-covered mountains

mountain pass
the last barrier
fog

muddy highway
the mountains
on the move

spring flooding
even the highest land
green

puddles
dried up
puddles covered with pollen
moiré shapes of shores

in puddles
the pattern of raindrops
dyes the hills green

spring sky
snow-melt puddles filling
to the brim

ridge
a spring day
someone young comes
from the ridge

jazz at the winery
Annapolis applause
ridge to ridge

music gathers
on soaring ridge tops
the distant haze

rivers
blooming
in the creek bottom
water

clouds
flooding the river
bubble sounds

flooded
the Russian River
watches us

flooded road
the sign slides
into the river

glub glub
the flooded river
drinking stones

rain
the river beginning
on the roof

spring
a river polishing
each rock

sunny skies
the mud-brown river
begins to shine

15

rocks

day shine
coming to low tide rocks
sea salt wet

in this house
the rock walls dream
of spring floods

just at dawn
the largest wave whitens
the rocks

rocks give way
dawn's light rolls over
eastern peaks

sea spray
a rock writes
another name

white waves
on the lava rock
leave it darker

sea

a quarter moon
the quicksilver sea smells
of old coins

breaking waves
dawn releases the light
over the sea

breaking waves
the sea cove fills
with mist

dawn gold
drawing lines on the sea
one for the horizon

heavy rain
the ocean is deeper
by a cloud

morning to night
in the embrace of change
calm seas

seaside
the other air
of a new face

seashell
the fluid around life
its own egg

sea light
swells and curls
to enter a wave

spindrift
the uneasy pillows
of sea memory

the open sea
a face still young stares
back at me

white waves
all the light in the sea
coming ashore

stones

moon meditation
in a glow of colors
the stone speaks

spring
when stones speak
of running water

tree stone
on its jagged edge
moon blossom

tides

low tide
the sea flattens for
a skipped stone

waves

incoming waves
the darkness curves
into the night

radiance
on the edge of water
this moment

SPRING Livelihood

arts

across her palm
the streak of green paint
a new lifeline

between his fingers
and the baby grand piano
the music

curtains part
the flower show begins
with bending sepals

musician playing
his hands so agile
on his wife

out of focus
in the camera's lens
a new face

photographer
in and out of focus
when it rains

roof leak
on the artist's sketch
watercolor by God

spring thaw
she is ready to return
to watercolor

rain or sunshine
unable to choose a weather
for the painting

babies

in my palm
a newborn's head
a luscious peach

dreams

open hands
the morning's dream
forgotten

cleaning

an open window
my desk cleared off
by spring wind

clean sheets
moon shine covers my bed
with new dreams

spring cleaning
the waterfall arranges
its rocks

clothes

make up
the ring around his collar
foreign lipstick

slipping into it
sun on a small-wave sea
my shiny dress

spring rain
my white dress dyed green
by the hills

spring softness
young mothers wearing
shorts

sweaters
still friendly
but unsold

sweat shirt
when he sees her in a pink one
he does

concerts
again music fills
every cell of still listeners
candle flicker

at the edge
of the outdoor festival
artists

breeze
a flutter of table cloths
petal shower

jamming
baby rocked to sleep by
dad's drum

music
going home
in cases

new age music
the clink of wine glasses
fretless guitar

on the table cloth
fluttering shadows
a second one

outdoor jazz
mountains exchange
the applause

overture
before the first act
it begins to rain

packing up
the chatter of musicians
snap their cases

taking home
an afternoon of music
sunburn

the murmur
around outdoor tables
the wine

eating and drinking
the moon fills
the empty tea cup
colder now

days linger
after dinner the light
on the tablecloth

flood waters
filling on a deserted island
a wine bottle

golden tea
my first night's
light dinner

munching chips
he says it sounds the same
as silkworms

room too large
candles flicker in the dark
of black tablecloths

wine glasses
fill and empty
with light

with my coffee
the sun breaks through
the fog

health issues
big bang theory
nine months later
she has a baby

hearing of abortion
the ear-shaped fetus
in the bucket

my mouth
not to be trusted
tooth fairy tale

twilights
surface of a deep lake
the birth caul

waxing moon
how it lingers on my leg
wearing a cast

housing and enclosures
going to bed
naked in my window
Venus

leaving the house
daffodils gather around
the doorway

locked gates
yet the blossoms have gone
away with the wind

skylight
a glow on green hills
tin roofed barns

the poems
a curtain billows before
an open window

waxing floors
sunshine slides
over the boards

play
a child's hand
rose to touch the sky
flying a kite

beachcomber
collecting early morning
in shells

by the window
you reading tantric texts
sparrows mating

doll clothes
remnants from my daughter's
wedding dress

first light
a shining in the teddy's eye
wakes the child

for what do they fish
the two young boys
in willow shade

jetting up
light in the darkness
of fountain water

married
to the wrong person
maypole dance

morning paper
evening stone
scissor light

painting the kite
blue
the color of home

spring joy
twigs dropped from the bridge
float to the other side

store-bought kite
his signs his name
and a happy face

wearing muddy boots
the boy flies in the sky
a pure white kite

transportation
escalator
faster than the moving stairs
the missed train

luxury liner
spring too comes to the island
for tourists

more stars
in Orion's belt
ocean liner

polluted
on the map my land
painted green

spring mud
tires spinning
a shower

spring traveling
a thousand miles of birdsong
only my two ears

without stopping
the hurricane passes over
the disputed border

writing and reading
a silver mic
above it his sweaty face
snow white nappy

a slow bass note
the evening slides from silence
into applause

applause scatters
the mood follows us
to the book table

blue skies
blue seas . . . blues . . . my dick
the drone of a poet

coastal fog
in a cup of tea and new book
Chinese paintings
-Yu Chang

in recognition
of poets moved far
their same voices

more books
slipping from the shelves
spring run-off

one small woman
shines out to tell us
touch someone

one thread pulls
individuals together
is she okay?

poems light up
on heaven and earth
our faces

reading
to the sound of rain
poetry

small jokes
lying flat on the floor
amplifier wires

so nervous
poets as non-poets read
non-poems

the bass
electrified by the musician
jazzes the audience

the haiku
writer hitches a ride home
passing calamities

work
gentleness of evening
her chapped hands twist
the wooly fleece

snow cranes flight
for a moment workers stop
building a sub-division

ukiaHaiku Festival
ukiaHaiku festival
only the ocean
is still

no wind
and yet I am to give
a speech

rolling on Hwy One
the ocean so still
only the car moves

unpatriotic
even the American flag
refuses to wave

Point Arena
on a sleepy Sunday
only flowers open

startled
the blackbird flies
into his song

before the speech
the nervous humming
of hymns

turning my gratitude
we're not on mountain roads
Malo Pass

going to the rez
the road lined with the red
of Indian paintbrushes

coming inland
the ocean's magnificence
as redwoods

coming inland
the depth of the sea
in redwoods

am old-new friend
grape leaves sprout
on open arms

climbing the pass
the huge white clouds
we can see from home

greeting an old friend
on outstretched arms
new grape leaves

meeting
at Church and School Streets
ukiaHaiku festival

clouds gathering
for the haiku meeting
all are nervous

too small room
overflowing with pride
parents and grands

children
reading their own haiku
all is perfect

the prizes
on the face of winners
a glow

applause
it carries us over
to next year

inspired
by his prize
a new book
        -for Armand

SPRING Animals

birds

a bird soars
where the air is clear
here you are

also green
the spring-flooded meadow
a snowy egret

bypassing death
the worm became a part
of the robin

darting
through the sleep of early light
swallows and dreams

dawn birds
a flotsam of flutes
tangle colors

eavesdropping
secret messages
as swallows fly

escaping
the overcast landscape
birdsong

evening settles down
the moor hen on her eggs
dew upon the grass

lifting my eyes
out of the coastal fog
osprey cry

out of a spring sky
small birds float into trees
light in their wings

pelicans are back
the rock-exposed cliff
is not so old

returning swallows
again my house
is home

sea gull wings
bringing the wind
to morning

sparrows
enter my ear
their chirping

spring
the flight of a bird
floats to earth

spring gulls
on the leeward beach
gathering wind

spring time
the caged bird sings with
the vacuum cleaner

spring traveling
a thousand miles of birdsong
only my two ears

starlings return
this spring melts into
all the others

sun after rain
warmth that invites worms
calls the robins too

thrush song
melting snow
into longer days

the little waves
of the spring sea
bird song

white sparks
from a bird's beak
the first notes

willow leaves
the kingfisher's blue drifts
into the fog

wind
catching on marsh grass
a bird's thin feet

without wings
stirring the blue sky
a metal crane

babies
adding anew
to the wooly fog
a lamb

among new lambs
the Canada geese huddle
in the sunshine

a new bird
not even in the book
the baby finch

barn kittens
shy but drawn to
spots of sun

breakfast
fat lips of baby birds
open the day

dotting the landscape
a flock of sheep
newborn lambs

eating breakfast
on a limb without hands
young osprey

ground fog
coming into winter
baby lambs

herb garden
the mint's scent of puppies
playing tag

highway ditch
the mortality lesson
as a dead fawn

home again
in the fish pond
tadpoles hatch

in fallen leaves
from last night's blow
a baby bird

litter box
the new kitten prefers
his shoe

mother's furry back
barefoot in the grass
puppies

nestlings learn to fly
at the same time sea oats
start to ripen

patting the window
the kitten discovers
stars

pink ears
shaped by cat cries
newborn kitten

pot sale
free to a good home
with a kitten

the burly plumber
sits on the kitchen floor
playing with a kitten

the ugly kitten
adopted first by my friend
the artist

tiger teeth
the kitten snarls
at the mirror

deer

dancing deer
raindrops in the woods
a sound of hooves

farm animals

evening
climbing a gentle hill
lamb and mother

ocean spindrift
taking shape in the meadow
a pregnant sheep

spring frost
in the near meadow
a white horse

sunshine
in the hen's beak
a voice

white waves splash
on the hillside
scattered sheep

frogs and fish

a spring day
toads being created
in my image

bullfrog
calls to
cowfrog

delicate pastels
in the pain of a pinch
from a crab

green into black
a frog enters
a snake's life

heron silence
landing in the middle
of frog silence

new moons
at the edge of the pond
fish milt

rain
in the frog's voice
the swamp

rehearsing vows
in the middle of the night
frogs

Route 575
so many frogs
so few haiku

silence
larger on the lily pad
a frog

sleeping in mud
for sex in the swamp
frogs

staring at the pool
from the tiled edge
a frog

the night
another color
frog chorus

insects that crawl
after dusting
the spiders seem at home
everywhere

coming out of the snail
coming out of the shell
his horns

flood lines
on the willows
a row of snails

squashing a bug
how the will to live
wiggles his legs

wooden
the Virgin Mary alive
with termites

insects that fly
deep flower
the bee enters
its own buzz

out of his buzz
the bumblebee lifts
a squiggly line

spring cold
in a half-opened flower
a bee warms itself

spring water
carried aloft
by bees

sunny day
the sky yellow
with butterflies

vibrations
petals opening
butterfly wings

wild lilac
a bush speaks
with bees

mice
sleeping over
at grandma's house
mice in the attic

taking refuge
behind the Holy Mother
a pregnant mouse

mating
chasing each other
Vivaldi's violins excite
mating birds

cliffs
shaping cloud shadows
two osprey

cockroaches
on the prowl for a mate
we bump

mating dance
kiss my buffy rump
swallows seem to say

on a spite fence
between feuding neighbors
cats in love

so busy courting
the two flickers fail to see
me coming

spring
migrating birds
pass me by

spring sunshine
even when it is dark
squirrels mate

tail held high
the young tom cat comes home
with a notch in his ear

nests
a flutter of wings
bridging the river
swallows' nests

a heart beats
in the shell
silence

a spring day
birds being made
in my image

church belfry
ascending swallows' nests
the prayers

church belfry
the swallows' nest
a holy of holies

high squawks
of the cypress grove
crow nests

leaving the rental
the arrival of swallows
in search of a nest

sacred spring
one prayer woven in
a bird's nest

shallow creek
coming to my eaves
swallow nests

silence
still in the nest
a waiting

solar eclipse
the cormorant continues
building her nest

sparrows
shopping for furniture
beaks full of grass

sundown still
a cormorant pulls dry grass
for her nest

sunset
a turtle lays her eggs
on this beach

the lease signed
we sublet the eaves
to nesting swallows

with wings
the hand-woven basket
a nest

pets
a lovely day
the cat leaves my work
to me alone

a new dog
the old couple younger
this afternoon

antenna
guiding the cat
his tail

barking at the rabbit
the neighbor's dog too
watches the moon

cat barometer
in the shape of his tail
opinions

flute holes
beside the cat
a striped tail

hoping to find him
hoping to not find his body
the missing cat

in the bush planted
on the tom cat's grave
a nest of wrens

kitty kitty
the morning air answers
with birdsong

morning cat
bringing in her life
the sun

night reduced
to a rush of rain
a purring cat

rainy day
the cat sits on the desk
in the *out* box

to stay inside
the cat sleeps curled
on all four paws

the missing cat
from every tree a cry
of spring birds

seals

a misty moon
harbor seals barking
at dawn

misty moon
harbor seals bark
as it nears

sinking into mist
harbor seals glide into
a gold-shot sea

snakes

blinded by scales
of the rattler's new skin
it strikes

whales

evening calm
smoothing the sea
where whales sleep

one mind
touched by the eyes
of a passing whale

sky-hopping whales
out to enjoy the sunny day
they remember

worms

cocoon
the worm wrapped
in moonlight

silkworm's cocoon
in three dimensions
a spider web

SPRING Plants

apple concert
a new depth
under the apple trees
alto sax solo

apple tree
through drifting clouds
new leaves

falling petals
the afternoon starts
with applause

filling the eyes
with apple blossoms
ridge top

fusion music
apple trees bloom
at the winery

getting lost
in apple blossoms
applause

in the break
notes from apple trees
petals

spots of beauty
under the apple trees
drum beats

the afternoon
rolling downhill
live music

blossoms
a blossom's dance
for the urges deep within
a silence

a change in the wind
the sunny spot receives
a drift of blossoms

almond blossoms
the bitter taste
when they fall

almond blossoms
the fragrance sweeter
with a waxing moon

a puff of smoke
wisps over the cottage roof
plum blossoms

blossoms
as if the spring haze is
their fragrance

cloud fire
on every tree
blossoms

evening glow
drifting away with blossoms
visitors' voices

light falls
from the evening sky
pale blossoms

misty rain
and the plum tree
bloom as one

not yet sold
the last plum bursts
into bloom

older now
even half a blooming tree
is enough

parking lot
someone has left
a blooming tree

plum blossoms
museum walls them
in and out

rain clouds
unfolding a budding moon
plum blossoms

reading something
in the spring wind
blossoms

spring blossoms
returning to the trees
with no memory

spring departs
leaving with the stone statue
scattered blossoms

spring fever
even the dried branch
blooms

suspected thief
I only wanted to see moonlight
on the blooming plum

talking together
the lilac covers itself
with blossoms

bushes
asleep in the woods
all the rhodie blossoms
wide open

blooming today
all the rhododendrons
I've ever seen

flowers on my path
overhead I find
wild rhodies in bloom

rain
raining rhododendron
blossoms

was it by chance?
today a bush and I wore
lilac

buds
deer-chasing bell
in the shadow of clanging
a rose bud

first spring rain
the sound in barren branches
of buds swelling

green womb
the flower to be
bulges a bit

holy pagoda
the first day
of the rosebud

inland
mimosa blossoms earlier
than our buds

late winter storm
the sun has receded into
primrose buds

leaving the house
daffodils gather around
the doorway

weather report
the crocus buds closed
against the snow

ready for flowers
day after day the bud
holds in itself

snow melt
expanding on bare limbs
swollen buds

that closed bud
on the phone I try
to say very little

bulbs
a little water
the will to live
as amaryllis

bud spear
winning the light race
higher than leaves

drawn to the sky
green from the earthen
amaryllis bulb

end of winter
a scent in the wind
crocus smell

in the cemetery
the biggest moon of the year
a hill of daffodil

leaving shape
pierces the bulb
bud spear

Safeway veggies
a pot of spring with
sprouting bulbs

spring dusk
coming from the hyacinths
the stay-awhile scent

sunshine
the yellow opens
a crocus

unseen red
the heart of a bulb
in bud

writer's block
the new amaryllis bulb
rough brown dried

cherry blossoms
a cherry tree
the house where spring lives
blossoms

among redwoods
drums dancers and flutes
cherry blossoms

back again
in the house of spring
cherry blossoms

black twigs
lost in cherry flowers
sins too disappear

cherry blossoms
staying awake all night
with friends

cherry wind
drifting from the trees
pink and white

coming home
again to cherry blossoms
always young

dawn
a new color comes
to cherry blossoms

dawn
misty light forms
cherry blossoms

face turned upward
cherry petals fall
on my cheeks

before the dawn
of cherry blossoms
fading stars

glowing hillside
the cherry blossoms' heart
of spring

high over a hill
cherry blossoms lift
a human heart

lipstick pink
touches a white shirt
cherry blossoms

night over
we stay for the dawn
of cherry blossoms

to the ground
that gave them life
cherry petals fall

with new wings
my heart flies up the mountain
of cherry blossoms

flowers
abandoned graves
spring leaves flowers
for a headstone

also a flower
as it curls upward
green sea

a whole day
with the opening flower
the things we don't think

colors flowing
from the abalone shell
sea side flowers

coming ashore
adorned with flowers
the boat of spring

early spring
sunshine-yellow flowers
in the ice plants

even in a flower
the female parts bigger
than the male

eye opening
where no eye has been
the flower

feeling shy
yet expensive lily-of-the-valley
demanded by the bride

history
how open was the flower
half an hour ago

into its buzz
the bee centers
the flower

listening
the flower opens
to other ears

May
a calendar of flowers
peaking each day

mists of May
covering the hillside
tiny white flowers

new life
in the withered fuchsia
a nest

no earthquake
yet a tremble opens
the white blossom

on my vacation
the amaryllis flower
grows two inches

opening slowly
the flower gives me time
to find it all

sepals lift
stamens and pistil curve
into awareness

silence
gathered into raindrops
flowers

spring fever
the rose blooms
just for us

spring haze
the flowers we see before
they bloom

sunlight
within the flowers
stamens lengthen

sweet alyssum
all of the gentleness
in lower case letters

thickest
along the unused road
forget-me-nots

unfolding
spring sunshine yellow
primroses

white ginger
the perfume I wore
when I was a virgin

white lilacs
carried like a baby
newborn scent

grass
a green haze
on yesterday's mud
grass sprouts

castle moat
flooded with daisies
new grass

it sways
as I ask the name
of a fragile grass

landslide
grass falls down
with its own earth

nest grass
flying through the rainbow
in the bird's beak

new green grass
the sun returns again
as blazing blades

someone breathing
at last in the cemetery
new green grass

spring flooding
even the highest land
grass green

string's melody
grass trembles
in the wind

tangled grass
high on the willows
flood lines

iris
an artist died
in the time of her blooming
iris

applause
sepals of the iris
unclapping

a roundness
pushing outward
the iris opens

arching
the iris opens
a rainbow

a ballerina
unfolding the iris
other music

blue ink
a letter not written
in the iris

closed gate
after the heavy rain comes
the prize iris gone

deep in the woods
where the sun rarely goes
a golden iris

eyes
enter the iris
opening

eyes
entering the iris
half-closed

eyes in secret places
deep in the purple middle
of an iris

folding paper
the faded iris
withers

iris blooms
leaving the clear calyx
its purple touch

iris blooms
the seventh one opens
differently

iris
the offering opens
a new flower

last night's lightning
today the iris and
the trembling

messages moving
without muscles
iris fragrance

moon eclipse
the growing light
white iris

never known to bees
the iris withers in rooms
of a maiden aunt

on a stalk
the butterfly wings
an iris

opening
the iris
the poem

ponds
slanted on the hillside
iris beds

pools of iris
refilled daily with flowers
sea meadows

sky
entering the iris
as it opens

shape-changing
in the witch's eye
an iris opens

silent butler
each day
a fresh iris

spreading sepals
one more poem
opens the iris

the iris opens
the furled flag
of other worlds

they stand so tall
the eye lifts to see
irises

wild iris
in a pool of praise
purple and gold

waiting with it
one iris withers
evening

windfall
the broken iris blooms
high in a vase

withering/blooming
on one straight stalk
iris

leaves
a branch brush
swirls on the paper
its own leaf

beech leaves
in a spring rain
a forest

fern leaves
unrolling the spoors
of memory

finding
first green tips of the rhubarb
now where's the recipe?

maple leaves
returning to the trees
as blossoms

new leaves
giving a sound
to the tree

opening leaves
covered with fine hairs
drizzle

outside
the old house
new leaves

too thin
to hold the full spring
trembling new leaves

leafy trees
a line of trees
down a rock fissure
a green river

anniversary gift
for the bare tree
new green leaves

being held
tenderly the light
in new birches

eastern melodies
the apple trees
newly planted

farm house
ancestor tree at the gate
leafing out

first light
the trees gather up
the darkness

from tree
 to tree
  tree music

in flower darkness
thick on the leafy boughs
raindrops

oak tree taller
we go to bed before
moonrise

old coast road
caught in the gullies
new willow light

sky high river
the alders out-flowing
the earth

spring
cracks in the ice
new trees

spring dawns
the leaves of fruit trees
bearing light

spring haze
a faint green gathers
in the tree tops

snow journey
from black trees
to water

the row in front
of the battered cypress
young trees

lily sequence
change of seasons
throws out the poinsettia
buys a lily

flower time
taking it to find
the lily

grace
before the meal
lily bud

breakfast over
the lily bud
is wider

snap sound
coming from the earth
the lily opens

morning alone
doing what we want to
the lily opens

watching the sea
the lily opens
to me

organ sized
the lily half-opened
in a sheath

the lily
awaking
me

puckered
as if for a kiss
the closed lily

waiting waiting
as if for a birth
lily still closed

yawning
stiff and tired of waiting
yet the lily opens

discussing god
above the table
the lily opens

unrolling itself
the half-opened lily
has a way to go

mouth
open in admiration
the lily

open now
letting the lily
face the sea

just for the lily
the Concerto by Vivaldi
for trumpets

lily deep
the eye travels
eons

swollen
with water I didn't drink
the open lily

pulling back sepals
to open the lily
unseen hand

before opening
inside this green room
I am the lily

forgetting its folds
the lily grows whiter
smoother

breathing deeply
before the opening bud
its fragrance

opening the door
so a bee may visit
the lily

across space
the lily opens
another star

two-fingers wide
the lily opens something
I know

bending sepals
the mystery opens
the lily

curving petals
the lily awakens
much

one petal
pushing another
the lily opens

half open
pistil and stamens
as if asleep

bending back
the white petals expose
a plump pistil

rolling back
to its beginning
the open lily

gull wings
folding and unfolding
the lily

the whole day
inside the lily
opening

it opens
with a tearing sound
the gentle lily

gentle lily
tearing itself open
to be a flower

open book
more answers
in the lily

tracing the lily
the pencil trembles
as does a petal

mother daughter
between them the lily
opening openings

messy! she says
clipping pollen-covered anthers
from the white lily

petals
cloud fire music
leaving under the trees
fallen petals

in the dirt
where petals fall
new flowers

listening
as petals fall
to the silence

music
covering the musicians
petals

petals
the candle flame lit
by spring

plants
jade plant
the tree for a Buddha
six inches high

pines
a couple whispering
on off-shore islands
the crooked pines

golden shade
under the redwoods
evergreen violets

new earth
under thick pine needles
a seedling

redwood sprouts
listening to the flutes
their own songs

redwood stump
with a rope tied around it
sprouts

shakuhachi tones
younger redwoods sway
first

water plants
water lily
home to the frogs
above and below

vegetables
a coolness
in the root cellar
potato sprouts

vines
passion flower vines
rising over the slat fence
flute notes

twined together
wisteria vines
blossoms

weeds
skunk cabbage
the smell of water
begins spring

uprooted by flood
smartweed hangs on the oars
of the rescue boat

SUMMER

SUMMER Moods

accepting
after visiting
her cozy garden plot
my smooth ocean

alone on the beach
letting the waves
come to me

blue jay
on the too-sunny porch
a noisy neighbor

cloudy day
waiting on the sunshine
to write my poem

summer sea fog
forgetting the phases
of the moon

the wide horizon
a ship crosses the line
without a poem

afraid
afraid of lightning
as a child and even now
as I grow old

anticipatory
avoiding waves
the excuse to touch
each other

first meeting
questions shove aside
the shy smile

sailor's wife
the twinkle in her eye
the sunlit sea

sultry night
her silk blouse clings
as if he touched it

wanting it to come
and the place it isn't
the next wave

angry
angry with him
yet how to write an ad
for someone else

crossing the bridge
all my anger
on the other side

dark figs
no smile in her
eyes

storm tide
the sea becomes
an angry person

you were so angry
yet I loved you even more
picnic showers

anxiety
alone on the rock
there seems to be something
the sea wants

growing uneasy
and then the wind drops
the beach fills

in the plane
the carpeting looks
the way I feel

nervous
the first of the rockets
wobbles

shivering
with cold and excitement
moonlit beach waves

storm gone
my urge to flee
passes

summer guests
it seems my job to make sure
the weather is nice

vibrating
the edges of my boundaries
go into the sea

wiggling
and then the atonal piece
changes

alone

alone and not alone
the warm beach
the rest of my body

all alone
the mountain sends down
a calm evening

alone on the beach
billions of tiny lives
and me

children gone
the moon sets into the sea
alone

married 35 years
even when I am alone
I am not alone

summer's night
leave the window open
or we'll be alone

the kayak shrinks
as the river widens
very much alone

wave after wave
one is never alone
on the beach

boredom

afternoon
the awning barely flaps
in the boredom

afternoon boredom
ants crawling
on the hours

afternoon boredom
the woman ties shells
on her straw hat

graveyard
bored with being solemn
kids play tag

returns
returning
turns

calm
a certain calm
in summer's passing
flowers

beach magic
the kids stop screaming
"look at me!"

breaking a string
worries and cares
left at home

calm
as the ocean is
I'm not

calm and warm
I float on the river
days later

flat seas
with the butterfly's flight
a certain calm

meditation
the bay is smoothed
by rising tide

on the beach
the exercise of demons
no longer necessary

sticky with sand
finally at home
in my skin

the hour silent
before the birds awake
waves on sand

untangled
the gift necklace
after the fight

cared for
friends
the pine tree sends me
some shade

shamanic journey
a red dragonfly comes
to guide the canoe

contentment
a summer's day
it has been good
even as it goes

back home
all the music
in the stars

going home
the tired way the beach
follows the sun-burnt

lying in the stream
at first it clouds and then
I am clear

needing nothing
I climb the hill
with an afternoon

river and sky
sliding into each other
hills and trees

summer sun
the whole world
is a friend

such simplicity
why can't I always live
in a summer house

sunset
warmed by flute music
my own heart

tied to the wind
a hum in the hammock
deep contentment

completeness
coming home
the full moon enters
a summer sea

gorgeous weather
all my summers
in this day

home again
my body in the creek
I float away

in groups
as if granite rocks
are families too

a photo
in her last letter
my thoughts

not sharing
root, nor form or gesture
just this day

on the beach
everything in the sea
goes back home

sun and surf
a day sandwiched
in our lives

together at the foot
the mountain and I share
one day

coping
afraid of lightning
the old lady relaxes
in the power

closing my eyes
the ceremony error
not seen

culture clash
American and Japanese
speaking German

deep thoughts
a tourist stops
to see the sea

eyes closed
my ears touching the night
with all seeing

screaming kids
nothing to do but play
my harmonica

tired muscles
in the evening chill
homeward bound

daydreaming
as if alive
the surf rolls a log
on the beach

a trail
to the sea horizon
her vision

defeat
art contest
knowing the pain
in paint

heated contest
blushes cooled outdoors
in reality

dizzy
dizzy
with the tilt of earth
high tide waves

dizzy
stars swing around the rim
of the sky map

doing the wild thing
it feels illicit
sleeping so close to nature
camping in the wilds

her Buddhist vows
yet now and again she thinks
of the fly swatter

eagerness
packing a picnic
into a big basket
nervous excitement

shivering
with cold and excitement
moonlit surf

ephemeral
a summer day
it has been good
even as it goes

just before sleeping
I was floating on the river
in my bed

summer's heat
a sun sparkles on the sea
and then it is gone

fear
even in a corner
the cat and I found
by lightning

so far from the sea
has my heart stopped?
the silence

vacation
the fear I have forgotten
how to write

feeling rich
breathing
in and out the tide
enriches the beach

for the rich
both sides of the freeway
decked with oleanders

forgetting
huddled on the beach
the sated woman forgets
she is a lady

staying on the beach
so long it forgets
I am here

friendly
lifting fog
the sea waves
I wave back

giving in
dinner time
the quiet voices
of hunger

if the sea wants it
letting my hat fly
off the cliff

jokes in Japanese
the handheld giggling
beyond me

moonlit beach
we let our footprints
wash out to sea

to just float
playing with the ocean
playing with me

shells
not picked up
worries too

the steep hillside
a wanting to give all
and let go

growing old
daydream
getting older it is
a nightmare

fading light
yet on her face
a warmth

growing old
with a boyish face
his summer hat

happiness
a great gift
a day on the beach
given to me

bird dress
wearing its colors
my heart flies

curve of a heel
rising with my happiness
waving grass

it comes
from her knees
the giggle

my friends
faces aglow with music
meeting them anew

same style
the blue dress worn more
than the black

summer fresh
my hair washed
in sunshine

healing
acupressure
the rocky beach nap
heals all over

healing
the miles my mind travels
without a step

idleness
idleness
casting stones in a pond
can this be wrong

increasing
afternoon tiredness
a foghorn

manifesting
the afternoon
yawns

low tide
my thoughts replaced
by empty sand

mountain wind
idleness stretches me out
on a sunny porch

nodding off
a stalk of grass taps
on my straw hat

romantic idea
yet all day I've lain
in the hammock

sleeping on the beach
the earth turns us all
into the sun

sleeping on a log
from summer to autumn
the river passes

stiff and sore
too tired to feel
the sunburn

swimming – yes
but in summer I'd rather
just float

taking a rest
I let the city noises
leak out of my ears

lonely
lonely
behind the fence
haiku

this house
with river stone walls
flows of loneliness

unable to leave
behind the cupboard
one knotted hair

longing

auto trip
the unspoken number
of things I miss

home safe
the granddaughter's call
full of longing

home sick
I have sailed the seas in ships
with of billowing clouds

homeward bound
all the words have turned
to pure longing

loss

love songs
in the flute player's face
grief

loving

August days
the warmth of young love
for the old guy

dreaming of you
the August afternoon grows
warmer

fireworks
in his eyes
our young love

his eyes
just looking at me
steal the poem

old songs
coming alive in August
April Love

river mouth
the lovers stop
for a kiss

sticky sand
the lovers draw
a part

sucking with all my might
so why do they call it
a blow job?

surprise
the old couple find
their hormones

summer novel
waiting until dark to read
the love scene

still lake
ripples of pleasure
when we touch

tucking in
the waist band of shorts
a book of love poems

words not spoken
when you fall in love
voice of the violin

oneness
barefoot
we are all equal
on the beach

pain
shakuhachi
in the half-notes
pain

panic
around the bend
wind and high waves
the panic

peace
floating
on August's slow river
my jade body

in summer
visitors north and south
my peace

original
beautiful when flawed
by the hum

mountain home
how quiet the woods
of old furniture

meditation posture
it is always the best
on the beach

play
playing with me
the kite
and its string
the simple toys

of a wide beach
everything new

praise
the beach remains
with or without me
this fantastic

transparent as glass
the flesh and bone tabernacle
the beauty about us

questioning
a beach of a day
asking why I don't
live here always

a summer's day
if bugs can be born again
why can't I

a summer day
if the sea exists
why can't I

have these rocks
chosen this view
or is it just luck

man or woman
far down the strange road
the argument

rising wind
will the fog clear to sunshine
before I freeze

what do they feel
redwoods listening to music
from bamboo

remembering
even when old
a bit of childhood recovered
by bare feet

on a sunny beach day
sand fleas on a straw hat
remembering rain

our weather today
not as good as last year
when you were here
           -for Joachim

sweet clover pie
the crust needs less sand-salt
and more mud

sun warmed
the smell of childhood
again an old woman

white socks
on smooth brown legs
1950s again

sad
our last day
all Japan becomes
a stage

such sad times
no one wears perfume
shaped as flowers

surf roar
unable to quell
the weeping

satisfaction
a new found night
shared with all the stars
all mine

barefoot
as before I was born
on the beach

by the sea
nothing made by man
nothing to ruin a life

closer to the mysteries
living along with the wind
in sea mists

existence
in mountain distance
silence

living by the sea
with those distances
in my heart

naked in the stream
all my hungers filled
by sun sparkles

my wealth
while lying naked in the river
sun pennies

old man
so proud of his many years
and new car

our days
dissolve into stars
drifting on beaches

sky sisters
the edge of heaven
touching the sea

shy
a shyness
as waves cover and uncover
my nakedness

sleepless
beside me
the cold side of the bed
awake

slowing down
a flower opens
in time-lapse photography
a bird extends a wing

soaring spirits
incoming tide
as my spirits soar
the beach narrows

thankfulness
a door torn away
into a small loss
gifts come

after a shower
how clean the beach seems
from the window

flotsam & jetsam
the beach is full of nothing
I have to clean

from a flute
a song to the river
as thanks

houses
anchoring the heart
in boxes

how small
next to the garbage can
my farts

sitting here
the far sea horizon comes
with thanks

a trail path goes
to the sea horizon
thanks to you

thoughtful
thoughts flying
out of the surf spray
feathers on my hat

understanding
anchored
by the rocks
spirit boat

a day
wading in the river
tonight my white hair

a summer day
for this I choose
to exist

beholding
the candle's light
my eye a world

bodies of water
in bodies of water
swimming

buying ice cream
to save the rainforest
someone snickers

even some rocks
seem to be female
everlasting

dowsing
suddenly the urge
to pee

each tourist
dressed in opinions
from home

if I were not here
between the notes
still flute music

listening
to the ocean's shell ear
hearing one's own

stuck in sand
shells and wooden sticks
are all my relatives

the earth
above itself
flowers

unhappy
guests
unhappy with the wind
that comes in gusts

unfaithful
slipping off
slipping off his wedding band
slipping off his sport jacket

unknown
her scoop neck
suddenly he is unsure
where to look

the stare
a line drawn
to the future

waiting
for the day to take us
to the unknown

worship
a boat in the sea
the sea within the boat
flowers

a servant of servants
a love-monument of mountains
is a holy wilderness

bride boat
pregnant with spirits
in flower shapes

even when dried up
vow-made waterfall is
still powerful

in the beginning
all spirit – all holy
a world boat

is it a kite
or is it a bird nest?
spirit house

to a beach of stones
we carry a boat of blossom
afloat with prayers

the ship
of ancestor offerings
ready to sail

wishes
canning tomatoes
if only this day could
be preserved

good wishes
the curtain billows
out the open door

worry
coming of summer
it brings the worry
will it be a good one

guests
each day I worry if the weather
will be nice

this round rock
how far from home
has it gone

SUMMER Occasions

arrival of summer
beginning of summer
the river so full
of vacation plans

beginning of summer
the deep days
of our friendship

first day of summer
opening the photo album
of childhood

summer again
sun pennies in the sky
of the river

August
August still
hot winds blowing away
the end of summer

back to work
it must have melted
my summer vacation

lovely days
fade and pass away
August again

shriveled with heat
the month of August
ends too soon

departing summer
a shriveled leaf
still hanging on
to summer's end

as summer passes
the golden grass waves
in its stiffness

departing summer
the street mime gets a round
of applause

dusk
at the end of summer
my coolness

end of summer
beyond the garden gate
mist turning to rain

end of summer
cows from high pastures
with flowers in their tails
Brigels Switzerland

end of summer
going inland
for jury duty

end of summer
in the cool morning air
at the open door

end of summer
ladies in bathing suits
on a wider beach

end of summer
one more wave
comes ashore

end of summer
the playhouse door
sags on its hinges

end of summer
the island of rock
stays in place

end of summer
tall and bright in the fields
of thistle

end of summer
without a birthday
I am older now

golden beach trail
grasses flat before
the end of summer

on a flat sea
the end of summer
wind still

summer's end
the rusty camp cot
becomes trash

summer passing
the path to the beach
where no one goes

dog days
the cat too
is much too hot
on dog days

Fourth of July
4th of July
fireworks reminding the men
of war

4th of July
fireworks the night
the condom bursts

after fireworks
a line of lights follows
returning cars

after the fireworks
the out-of-towners leave
roadside trash

besides fireworks
we get to see
our neighbors

boom!
the dark lets out
the fireworks

bright stillness
after the fireworks
the smoky wind

Christmas in July
fireworks twinkling
through pine trees

downwind
of the fireworks
a black smell

fireworks
caught in the clink
of ice cubes

fireworks done
still seen in darkness
the dream

59

fireworks
the picnic potato salad
gone bad

fireworks' finale
the dome of lights
still stars

fireworks finale
out of the darkness
the width of stars

flowers of the night
celebrating the freedom
of fireworks

freedom
released into the night sky
fireworks

growing darkness
the fireworks brighten
until they fade

Independence Day
instructing my daughters
how to invest

in the cove
jellyfish float below
fireworks

on the fourth of July
beads burst from a necklace
fireworks

outdoor holiday
a shower and the glow
of sun burn

over the sea
fire works slowly followed
by the boom

rattling the house
before the fireworks
boom of the wind

red white and blue
the setting moon in the glow
of fireworks

sea fog
the fireworks appear
fuzzy

silent
fireworks
the new moon

six miles from town
after the colors fade
the boom

small town
the fireworks begin
late

sunset glow
fading before the fireworks
moonset

sweeping
smoke from fireworks
lighthouse beacon

the neighbor's pine
taller this year the fireworks
seem shorter

tired of waiting
for the late fireworks
the new moon

waiting for darkness
the sea continues to glow
without fireworks

waiting for fireworks
a faint globe shines
a slender moon

waiting for fireworks
first the paper grows dark
with ink

waiting for fireworks
the only flares are on
sun-burnt skin

summer passing
the only brightness
in summer's passing
flowers

a cool wind
summer passes
before it begins

holes in the lawn
looking for a snake
the end of summer

late in summer
the fountain overflows
with coins

late summer
even hotter by the breath
of dragonflies

mid-summer
the sadness of knowing
days grow shorter

summer days
framed by hands
of kelp and stone

summer solstice
a bluish shadow
our shortest night
in Norway

mid-summer's eve
my trip around the sun
is half-done

midsummer madness
tempered by the knowledge
each day is shorter

solstice splits
between the peach halves
a red stone sun

summer solstice
the gypsy wagon bright
with music

walking the fence
with arms outstretched
summer solstice

SUMMER Celestial

breezes

cliff meadows
fragrant flowers named
by sea breezes

cool as a visitor
sea breezes inland sound
in the trees

following the path
to come in the door
a summer breeze

hiking through
on tops of sea meadows
the scented breeze

morning breeze
coming in the window
surf sounds

shall it be cool
or will it be warm
summer breeze

sunset's blue colors
from deep in the forest
a cool breeze

the only visitor
in the Sunday gallery
a summer breeze

trees sway
the performers blessed
by evening breezes

such flowers
as large as the sea
water fragrance

tapping my shoulder
the low branch tells me
of a cool breeze

the shape
of shore pines
a cool breeze

the way water
walks into the canyon
a cool breeze

white cloth
pinned to a clothesline
rising with coolness

wind chimes
the silence absorbs
any cool breeze

clouds

cloud country
above the smooth sea
hills and valleys

cloud cover
the shadow of hours
still dark

cloud crowd
chased from the beach
by sunless cold

cloud furniture
moving in all sorts
of weather

clouds
the flowers springing up
in sky fields

clouds dissolve
in the setting moon
is it that hot

clouds
of long ago coming
from the hill

clouds melt
old poems called it
summer rain

clouds with air streams
appearing above the mountains
floating fountains

coming together
evening clouds and
the flute players

crossing the canyon
footprints of the wind
as clouds in the sky

dotted with sea foam
the very small beach holds
summer clouds

down to earth
white clouds floating
in rocks

drum music
written in the clouds
white and blue

growing slowly
over golden sea meadows
summer clouds

inland clouds
the tops of big waves
in blue sky

mountain afternoon
holding up the sky
columns of clouds

stained
by not-dropped rain
a sea of clouds

sunlit cloud
the illuminated heart
of a floating body

the faraway land
of mountains by the sea
cloud peaks

the full moon sinks
into our small clouds
heaven on earth

traveling
the seas in ships with sails
billowing clouds

over a summit
the cloud continues
as a mountain

whispering peace
our first mountain day
warm calm cloudless

white water rivers
rising first as mountain's
thunderheads

wispy clouds
a white-water view
of the sky

under construction
cloud pillars of the temple
with sky roof

comet
a shooting star
the arc in the sky
made by my eyes

a wry neck
a moon eclipse
and a comet

radiating
neck pain trying to see
the comet
                    coolness
a day shortens
as the beach cools
its shadows

concert
the stillness outdoors
cool

cool in summer
hanging in the hammock
under shade trees

cool untouched
by human hands
summer morning

dry creek bed
a coolness flows down
evening

early morning
the little night of coolness
leaves the shadows

evening coolness
on a low-tide beach
small waves

evening coolness
remakes the canyon rocks
drops to the river

floating on air
that's never been too hot
early summer

low notes
the cooling in the woods
smells strange

sweet air
night comes down the canyon
in its coolness

taking off a raincoat
as if to keep the coolness
for later

waiting for the moon
a gift from the darkness
is a cool wind

wind chimes
the silence absorbs
any cool breeze

dawn

dawn comes
with the beach empty
of footprints

lifted free
at dawn's edge
the sun

organdy curtains
billowing from the window
morning glow

slowing
early morning light
one cicada

warmer now
the sky page fills
with ink

darkness

darkness
coming from the flute
the low notes

near darkness
the whole world held aloft
by one tree

summer eve
the concert ends
before dark

dew

seaside gardens
summer dew comes filled
with ocean power

drought

drought
the cracked mud patterns
on the giraffe

drought years
the rock garden filled
with shimmering stones

for months
the only sound of rain
in the wind

lawn sprinkler
stilled and dusty
a prayer for rain

summer drought
the dust-covered brush
leaves no trace

evening

evening moves
in the mountain church
a dark-toned bell

evening
another of those
by-gone days

nearly evening
beside me in the sand
chilly shadows

play ground
the cool slide
into evening

seaside cliffs
at one with the same
evening glow

sunset's rays
striking the bell
of evening skies

fog
a band of fog
sun strikes a wave
as a flute

breathing deeply
in the steep ravines
clouds of fog

buoy bell
the shape of the fog
evening

evening
in a secret cove
fog bound

evening fog
a door slams softly
against the dark

fog coming in
over the low rock
a white wave

fog feathers
the blue sky comes
with the wind

foggy day
all the words are
in the sky

foggy morning
all my new poems
are memories

fog
the weird face in the rock
seems gentle

high tide
the afternoon disappears
in fog

islands of fog
blotting out the land
evening

leaving the nest
and scattered by wind
fog

low fog
elevated by swallows
moving islands

morning fog
putting out all the colors
the sun

morning fog
the beach shrouded
in its day

morning fog
the dream written down
still alive

out of the fog
doing meditation to the sun
it comes to a cliff

sea sky blue
between islands of fog
late afternoon

shaping the fog
shaping the coast
sun-warmed seas

softening the world
so texture disappears
summer fog

summer sea fog
forgetting the phases
of the moon

sunrise
the fog holds up
a pale plate

the land of seas
expanding into summer
ocean fog

tourists complain
my home-like feelings
for ocean fog

waking slowly
the ocean still covered
with summer fog

wide world
in summer fog the sea
becomes the sky

wind chimes
as fog blows away
the sound of sun

heat
a vanishing bird
the heat of summer
goes with it

body temperature
the beach shimmers
with heat

don't believe them
it has nothing to do with water
the heat wave

dreaming of you
the August afternoon grows
warmer

gliding inland
sea sparkles whiten
afternoon heat

heat
the fragrance of star light
jasmine

heat wave
even the fat ladies show up
in shorts

heat waves
her body shivers
in candlelight

hot dry air
valley memories
of my marriage

in the camera
the heat of the day
in pictures

in the heat
a sky emptied of color
clouds and flowers

into the heat
the display canon fires
smoke

magnetic fields
drawing inlanders to the sea
these hot days

noon-time heat
blue in the evening shadows
of the rocks

open doors
the heat comes out
with music

slanting the heat
of the late afternoon sun
new tin roof

summer heat
pushing down to the water
my face

summer's heat
a sun sparkling on the sea
and now it is gone

summer
a copper kettle
on a stove

the heat
a kimono open
to a breeze

too hot to clean house
too hot for anyone to notice
just too hot

waiting lures
the leaden weights
of summer heat

warming my ears
more than any breeze
the flute master

light
adding to the day
the roundness of extra hours
summer light

deeper in rock
past and future twist
colored light

evening light
coming ashore
atop the waves

wind
filling the sails
with light

lightning

lightning
a glimpse of the other
life I live

steeple
on its pointed tip
lightning

long day

a long day
so much to do
yet grass to cut

farther away
these long days
at high noon

longer days
I love to go to sleep
with sky in my eyes

long day
the reading lamp stays
unplugged

Milky Way

drunk too
this night of stars
the Milky Way

not yet sour
in the night sky
the Milky Way

the River of Stars*
hangs over the sea
sky sisters

*Japanese term for the Milky Way

mist

just wind
in the sea mists
closer to mysteries

misty white
the land of the fog's
sea shore

morning mist
the scent of roses
from a bush

sea mist
drawn to the moon
incense smoke

sitting here
the sea horizon comes
as mist

white mist
the oldest visitor
at the sea shore

moon

an invitation
to walk on the curved beach
new moon

balanced
the full moon leaves
earth to dawn

day gold
silvered by moonlight
dried grass

even shorter
the summer night
with a full moon

first fireworks
moon shine broken
by a wave

full moon
marking in beach sand
footprints

high seas
how can they say it's waterless
the lowered moon

how loud the surf
filled with moonlight
high and round

how rich the sky
velvet with a full moon
and shining Venus

into the sea
with the full moon
only Venus

it disappears
with clean glasses
a misty moon

mid-day
moonlight lingers in the sky
as bright shadows

moonlight
another accessory
for the new house

moons
fade and pass away
August again

morning moon
the day's journey starts
so slender

narrow
yet so silver is the sea's
path of the moon

over the Pacific
the full moon hangs as if
lonely for the sea

the bright moon
has gathered up the stars
into itself

the slender moon
on a rose petal curving
before it fades

walking to the beach
on the path the moon
goes ahead

warming the moon
the red-tipped glow
of incense

women rediscover
a calendar of moons
in his story

moon rise
a morning moon
strings up the planets
I dreamed of beads

moon set
countless times
the moon has set
a calm sea

face to face
the late setting moon
rising sun

out of the clouds
the setting moon appears
larger – closer

night

nightfall
the roar of the sea
darker

nightfall
the sea resists the darkness
of land

nightscape
the many shades of color
which have no name

short nights
my dreams of you last
into the day

shortest night
the darkness dissolves
in moon brightness

still seas
blue of the coming night
in smooth water

summer nights
the swimming pool warmer
than the dark air

swinging
the garden gate
day and night

tropical night
the sky of a warm wind
dark velvet

rain

bending without wind
the green leaves accept
a sudden shower

driving into wood
the roundness of raindrops
and then the shine

eager for summer
yet another week of cold
rains

early summer rain
in the mountains someone else
eager for a vacation

entering summer
slowly through the door
of the rainy season

fallen petals are sad enough
the coming of the rainy season
drowns all my hopes

getting smaller
as the far mountains
end of the rain

heavenly
the soft ring of rain
becomes the view

it's raining
the earth and I
in damp joy

leaden skies
the drops of rain
are only fog

missing you
I walk naked
in a gentle rain

rain
blessing the earth
with thunder

rain glow
after dark I feel it
on my face

rain
touching the stone
holy clicks

rain showers
on the grassy field
dew and moonlight

rolling thunder
the just-missed bus takes
the rain with it

sparkles
on the summer sea
raindrops

summer rain
my only blanket
woven boughs

welcoming the spots
on my new cotton dress
summer rain

world greening
every rain cloud
leaves its mark

rainbow

after seeing many
I'm not sure they exist
– rainbows –

boom the wave
crashes into the cove
hanging a rainbow

flower colors
in the newly-seeded garden
a rainbow

sky

a brown wing
over the temple
a deep sky

a pink sky-sea
blanketing the low moon
as day begins

canyon stream
dried to a slit
of clear sky

children's voices
the sky arches itself
above them

clear blue skies
the ocean overturned
into a peace

colors of a day
puddles of sky left
by the sea

evening skies
first and last the lights
stars / jasmine

get-well card
behind the good wishes
blue sky

in the heat
a sky emptied of color
wilts the flowers

laughter
arcing into the sky
the summer day

looking to the sky
the musician conceives
the next drum solo

reflecting
a lighter blue than the sky
brown sand wet

sky cloud mountains
in pearly hills and dales
streams take their rise

sky edge
where the wear and tear is
my day

sky making clouds making sky

sky lake cold
pours into the window
sea fog

sky white
with heat only waves
come ashore

the sea waves up
to the edge of heaven
sky sisters

the sky blue
with dragon flies
stitching air

the sky curved
the rise and fall
of the tides

wind still
colors of the evening skies
lingering

south wind

a change of heart
in the sunset's fading colors
the south wind

south wind
the sea slopes
into its sound

stars

a gentleness
warming the night air
summer stars

at dusk
they shine out one by one
flowers / stars

climbing rapidly
Venus overtaken
by the dawn

early morning
the stars still humming
jazz riffs

earth fires
in the mountains
made of stars

how deep our sleep
in the mountain's heart
beneath stars

incandescent
a sky of shooting stars
volcano cinders

on the beach
some of the stars
are shells

out to pee
a sprinkle of stars
and a small sound

pointing
toward the fireworks
Venus and Saturn

stars
sky lilies above
valley dust

the sky bends down
to flat sea meadows
summer stars

storm

a thunderstorm
with an applause of wind
is over

rain stopped
the storm is not over
'til the power's on

twister!
afraid to watch the sky
afraid to move

sun

a glint of sun
blue skies brighten
the water

a spot of sun
moving over the hammock
breezes

a round rock
the sun slides
into the sea

between seasons
sun and shadow contain
hot and cold

bleached
by the rocky sun
bent wood

circling around
the beach umbrella
sun and its shade

curve of the sun
the road winds through
light and shadow

from branch to branch
the arched sun measures
hammock hours

hard
on the sea
sun

highest tide
as the sun set
the launched boat

hot sun
at the river's edge
my shadow melts

iced tea
in bubbles on the lemon
the sun

it ticks
the clock I cannot see
in a blaze of sun

leaving the beach
the tired way the sun
fills the tracks

melted
under the burning sun
the shadows

sharp
in the riffles
bits of sun

summer sun
dies into firewood
its true self

summer sun
it is not the same star
we had all winter

sunlight
streaming in the Blue Canoe
chamomile tea

sunny days
the flute with my breath plays
a lively tune

sunshine
crossing over the pond
on a bridge

sun warmed
holes in the hammock
still cool

the day begins
with the sun and moon
my breathing

the sun goes
from branch to branch
as hours

the sun rises and sets
in the northern bedroom
mid-summer

top of the pass
the rays of the sun
already there

to the sun
a summer afternoon
naked

sunrise
sunrise
following the mountains
over and again

sunset
after sunset
the light comes down as
evening showers

conversation
of flutes at sunset
the wind

day closing
a wave explodes
against a rock

drums
shadows begin to dance
at sunset

island music
at sunset the coolness
in the high notes

sunset
deeper the flute
warms us

sunset
in and out of clouds
again and again

sunset
music colors
in the clouds

the day's heat
sinking into the sea
the setting sun

the drawn line
tapers then to fade
sunset

the sun sets
now the waves
are really big!

writing it down
the poem about sunset
— it's gone

sunshine
essence of childhood
once a year the pure joy
of summer sunlight

rain predicted
how sweet the sunshine
we got instead

saddle-back
sunshine lines the ridge
with flying manes

sunshine
with the breeze from the sea
cooling

sweet waters
last gift to the sea
sunshine

thunder
distant thunder
high tide in the cove
filled with sunshine

on the horizon
rolling mountains move
the thunder

twilight
nautical twilight
the sea gives its last light
to the sky

twilight
among early stars
sea bird's cry

warmth
the year slows
and expands with warmth
summer

warmth
on a south side of a rock
afternoon

winds
a gust of wind
when the door slams
someone's *oh*

already blue
the cool wind
from the sea

coming to enjoy
our cool northern climes
the south wind

high winds
moonlight smoothes
rough seas

raising dust
and our hopeful spirits
summer wind

sun pennies
cold winds rattle
the August sea

telling the wonders
of the upper mountains
the night wind

the cool wind
now part of the day
at the beach

thermals
drawn by a circle
of birds

the shadow bends
blowing sand lengthens
evening

the wind comes
from across the sea
looking for a home

tornado scare
grandma teaches the kids
to make pinwheels

waiting
for the wind
sails

wind
taking water from one thing
into another place

wind thickened
into water white becomes
spindrift – afternoon

only wind
the watch-kitty closes
his eyes

a cool wind
in a dry creek bed
shivers

wind menu
smoke from the neighbor's
barbeque

wind
breathing life blood
into the flute

wind
the black flag
takes no notice

unable to sleep
in such a wind
new ideas

SUMMER Terrestrial

beach

a cat on a book
the way we walk on a beach
unable to read

at the beach
every haiku written
by the sea

beach secrets
where the sunlight hides
the blue in shadows

boom-boom beach
on the fourth of July
water-filled coves

day begins
with the beach clear
of my footprints

going home
the tired way the beach
follows the sun-burnt

holy grounds
on the Kona beach
smell of coffee

my favorite beach
driftwood too comes
ashore here

on the beach
things from the sea
going home

planning a trip
yet my feet take me
back to the beach

rolling r's
the voice of the sea
on a rocky beach

shell fragment
the whole beach
in its shape

summer
the little waves full
of beach

the beach
humming a song
without words

the long beach
           too short
we retrace our steps

the sea slopes
and beaches dry
south wind

wave upon wave
the beach is born
out of the sea

canyon

a strip of stars
above canyon walls
endless space

canyon walls
thunder and lightning
making them new

canyon walls
thunder rolling mountains
of red stone

flowing down canyon
into the dry river bed
evening cool

slot canyon sculptor
stone chips left fallen
by the river

sunspots
deep in the canyon
sand stone circle

caves
animal pictures
on cave walls
stone shapes

cliffs
afternoon sun
stepping down the steep cliff
shadow stairs

at home
the cliff makes a cave
for the boat

atop the cliff
the bay spreads itself
at my feet

cliff edge
showing the world
in clear water

cliff edge
the red moment
before birth

cliff shadow
the falling stone sends me
back into the sun

eroded cliffs
at every stage a person
in profile

high tide
the cliff shadow
disappears

pop!
the cliff gives me
a small stone

old river bottoms
rise up in the sea as
cliffs of history

sea cliffs touch
soft edges of water
nights

taking sunshine
into a secret cove
steepest cliffs

creek
in the creek
I the rock I am
home again

summer creek
the fish in me getting
fish kisses

summer-hot hills
folding together
dry creek beds

wading in the creek
with the first shock of cold
summer begins

without a boat
crossing the creek
pine shadow wind

desert
desert
awakened by silence
filled with dark

stars
in the sand
desert gift

your voice
tying me to the desert
toast pops up

earth
earth
moving into the sky
flowers

earth bones
smooth and washed bare
stone age

earth holes
slender from the sides
of snakes

eternal change
earth mesa rock
pebble tree

day heat
pulling loose
cracked earth

light changes
the ochre earth
in dried grass

sky world
drawn from earth
a line of trees

earthquake
nothing moves
miles from the earthquake
afternoon stillness

fields
fields of poppies
how far we walked to get
sun-burned noses

stretching out
over a summer field
my love for you

hills
bumpy road
hills in the drawing
covered with pines

climbing the hill
a bent pine and I
look over the bay

climbing the hill
a woman's shrill laugh
higher

coming home
gray clouds touching
sere hills

hills
in the sky
clouds

into the hills
losing the mountain views
to a curvy road

late afternoon
the melodies older
than the hills

naming the hillside
warm yellow flower month
the heat

one last rain
as the hills warm
to turn yellow

out of the fog
at the top of the hill
breathless sunshine

sea blue
the stacks of hills
come to the water

slat by slat
climbing the hillside
redwood fence

still fireworks
on the coastal hills
lighthouse beam

the hill
raises up the road
curves around it

walking slowly
the hills still covered
with summer fog

with distance
the hills arrange the fog
shades of blue

year-round fireworks
flashing from hill to hill
lighthouse beam

yellow hill
with overcast skies
it is sunny

island

a bird calls
morning light comes
to an island

afternoon breezes
the log island moves
against the current

day comes
to the islands
one by sun

deeply moving
between rock islands
sun-sparkled water

island music
coming inland
by the river

one log wide
the island deepens
the river

sea setting
a stone cathedral
in island cove

lagoon
bridge
at the edge of the lagoon
the wind stops

lagoon
the name makes kayaks wiggle
with laughter

lakes
prayers for rain
in the ear of the lake
its blue listening

ripples
the lake ear listening
to us

rough
the surface of the lake
pushes the wind

sunny lake
the canoe cuts the water
into light and dark

land
calm seas morning
the edge of the land extends
to the horizon

lifting fog
the land
    lands again

landslide
a chilling sound
rocks tumble down
from canyon walls

letting in the light
the steep slide of shale
lands aslant

rock hard
and yet so moving
the ancient flow

lava
earth burnt
by shadow black
shapes of lava

lava island
the sea once let the earth
blaze forth

meadow
flattened by heat
the meadow stretches
to the horizon

hiking
the scented breeze
of sea meadows

seaside meadows
summer dew comes filled
with ocean power

shiny waxed floors
that distance from
the grassy meadow

mountains
a line of yellow
pushing the mountains
into the sky

all alone
the mountain sends down
a calm evening

by the sea
mountains brought down
by my eyes

carrying us upwards
to their cool spacious abode
summer mountains

earth fires
in the mountain
made of stars

in the mountains
our ocean waves to us
as white clouds

mountains
moving the distance
between sounds

mountains and plains
exchanging in their years
places – spirits

mountain afternoon
the distance between sounds
grows warmer

mountain dew
the drops of sunlight
chilled

mountain ravine
a river of rocks
in the drought

mountain ravine
oaks grow together
in the stillness

mountain sunrise
I've seen the earth gather
up its shadows

remote mountains
the sky comes down
into stillness

tunnel
inside the mountain passes
through me

paths
every new leaf
makes it smaller
beach path

flagstones
music smoothes
the path

mountain road
twisting and turning
into a path

pool
resting
from ocean and river views
a tiny pool

ridge
top of the ridge
the sun follows
a curvy road

river
a fallen tree
the river returns
to itself

afternoon
sending shadows
down the river

beginning of summer
the river so full
of vacation plans

below the cliff
huge boulders swimming
in the river

blonde grasses
the green-eyed girl
is only a river

cascading river
lace-like sheets braided
over folding currents

dry riverbed
in one of its rocks
dreamless sleep

flowing
above the river
a wing tip

from his flute
a song to the river
from a master
                        - for Riley Lee

Gualala River
called by a flute
mosquitoes

here high
and over there low
the river banks

how it slows
to gather the algae clouds
summer river

leading the eye
to white in the sky
the cloudy river

Milky Way
the river bends itself
to the same path

oar shine
dipped in the river
sparkles

only smiles
my nakedness in the river
wrinkled

river
above the river
fog

river
flowing heavenward
in the trees

rocky river
the blue tongue
of God

spring cold
the autumn river
on a hot day

standing rock
the land's monument
to itself

summer clouds
floating in the river
billows of moss

sun glare
even the river pales
to a greenish blue

sunlit dew
riverbed gravel stands
out clear

the river way
a canoe divides
the sun

the road dips
down to a bridge
the river

water exchange
tree green moves
into the river

upside down
the river the world
of reflection

young again
bare feet dangling
in the river

roads

bumpy road
the shapes of the drawing
out of control

bumpy road
the drawing of hills
becomes pointed

down the road
the mountain and one
of its rocks

going higher
the mountain road disappears
into a cloud

muddy road
the mountains
on the move

social event
everyone at the turnout
for fireworks

twisty mountain road
going east I thought
yet the full moon's ahead

rocks

a plan
the sweep of water
carves a rock

a crack
in the monolith
one star

all around us
the anniversary celebration
3 million years of rocks

a secret
held by a rock
the black hole

august rock
leaking enough water
for a paint brush

basalt outcropping
the only flowers in this dryness
are red lichens

calling a name
waves on a rocky shore
with a mouth of stones

carved rock
the sea wave follows
hollows

chipped rock
the shape of water
falling

colors
from the give and take
of rock shadow

evening sun
gilding the rocks
with silence

evensong
rocks covering themselves
with darkness

flesh colored rock
it too has known
hard times

high noon
exposing the round rock
its perfect shadow

high noon
rocks patiently waiting
for night fall

hot day
a small rock from the cliff
plunges into the sea

leaving a sign
of a spirit's passing
holy rock

mountain shadow
only the rocks at sea
are sun bright

off-shore rocks
in rain-streaked windows
more jagged

on the beach
old eggs of the sea
rounded rocks

painting pictures
on smooth rocks
bubbling water

pointing
even round rocks tell
of the tide's pull

roaring
in the rock-hiding water
all those devas

rock forms
in the dried mud
rock forms

rocks in place
holding the image
of visitors

rock spire
fastened to its base
is a strong shadow

rounds
the many miles to make
the rock smooth

sea stories
told by faces of rock
wave lengths

sea swells
the low rock grows
and disappears

settling into blue
cliff-side rocks prepare
for night

slow afternoon
all the rocks decide
to stay right here

stained dark
again the sea washes
island rocks

the necessity
of a wave breaking
rocks

water faces
in the rock
carved dry

upward thrust of rock
tearing the blue silk sheets
surf sounds

upwelling rocks
pearly clouds of mountains
solid looking

wind and rain
carving new temples
in the rock

underfoot
the ocean rearranges
its rocks

yellow rock
moving toward the light
a shadow curve

sand

a sand beach
comes and goes with waves
of tourists

cold sand
hugging my back
to get warm

full moon
sand marked with bare feet
between waves

making angels
shapes in the smooth sand
from lovers

meditation
my butt finally at home
in the sand

raked sand
fireworks change
their patterns

sand and sea
the restless colors
in a flower field

sand giggles
the pattern of waves
left by ebb tide

wavy sand
the sound of water
changes its pattern

sea
a flake of sky
glinting in the sea
sun pennies

a fog bank
the cold blue seas
of molten metal

another human error
the only local intelligence
in the sea's wisdom

boats on your back
the longing to follow them
in the white water

calm seas
the boat pushed home
by twisted water

distant hills
wave after wave
into the sea

evenings
the ocean is always here
when I get home

flat seas
the weight of fruit
at harvest

foggy dawn
uneven the ocean tosses
spume and spray

hammock view
swinging back and forth
the sea and me

having given up waves
storms and dashing spray
in the summer sea

holy shells
ground down by the sea
jewels

it's so hot
the sun has melted
the metallic sea

moonset
the sea turns pink
with dawn

ocean view wealth
the sea shining with
sun pennies

on the horizon
lying down together
sea and sky

salt stained
teary windows overlook
the sea

silk soft
the force of the sea
moving rocks

silver sea
painted by the gold
of a setting moon

smoothing the sea
sunset's metallic gold
hammered flat

soft summer day
the way the sea rises
to meet the rock

a long day
evening comes finally
across the sea

yellow pink
my friends for a day
sea colors

shore
closer to shore
each thing becomes
what it is

rutted by landslides
the shoreline highway curves
into the sea

waiting for fireworks
the wind blows the darkness
along the shoreline

spindrift
small clouds
capping wind-tossed seas
spindrift

spindrift
the uneasy pillows
of sea memory

stones
beach nap
the afternoon covers me
with stone shadow

eons of sand stone
recording the flow
of yesterday's rain

moonset
where the water was
a white stone

slick rock
the wave that wetted it
cast in stone

words of god
spoken softly by
river stones

stream
in the distance
banks of the stream and I
come together

mountain stream
its coolness in me
goes into the day

surf
crashing surf
inland among the birches
a gurgling stream

curled water
coming unrolled
gentle surf

tidal flats
tidal flats
little rivers of green
light our boat

tides
a call not heard
something in the sea
returns the tide

a distant roar
the tide turns
to come to me

at high tide
a sudden noise
rock fall

coming to the beach
for a tranquil day
rising tide

ebb tide
her death touches me
with more loss

falling tide
before the stone dries
rain

full tide
afternoon sky leaves
the bay

full tide
coming ashore
coolness

high tide
the bay bigger by two
less rocks

high tide noon
the empty sea cave
sounds

high tide
fog too moves into
the cove

high tide
the centuries
low tide

high tide
the ocean comes
when I call it

high tide
the kelp bed
a blue wave

high tide
up the beach path comes
a child

low tide
on every rock
its face

low tide
only the sky fills
the bay

low tide
the light comes ashore
in small waves

low tide colors
night begins to dry
along the edges

no longer empty
the beach with my oldest love
high tide

rising tide
another rock
hides

smells
from the body of water
low tide

steps to the sea
each tide leaves a mark
another day

the day curved
the rise and fall
of the tides

the earth turns
rocks grow shorter
in the rising tide

with a roar
the tide turns
darkness

very low tide
rocks make a path
to the island

tide pools
tide pools
deeper now
with clouds

valley
alone in the valley
the sun stays on top
of the mountain

deeper into the valley
the snow atop the Sierras
only gets hotter

evening cool
follows the valley
to the river

valley floor
land so flat we need
no map

wide valley
the trees on the other side
are bushes

volcano
lava toes
finding a path
from the volcano

earth fires
of the molten mountain
melting again

waterfall
the giggle
a summer waterfall
hiding in the rocks

resting
the finger-wide waterfall fills
my straw hat

waves
avoiding waves
the excuse to touch
each other

breaking waves
a child throws a stone
at the sea

evening mist
the day's crashing waves
going to heaven

high summer waves
the water bottle floats
away

ink black rocks
with a thousand waterfalls
the wave passes

offering themselves
to the lopsided moon
crests of waves

the long day
on the sea waves
worn flat

sunset hues
waves the color
of mist

watching waves
breathing in and out
flute air

waves awash
as if to entertain me
one goes higher

wave washed
the grace of people
watching the sea

white and frilly
wave after wave
skirts the rock

white caps
deep enough
the ocean covers a rock
with small white waves

partly cloudy
the blue of the sea
with white caps

SUMMER Livelihood

arts

adobe walls
drawing red rock mountains
with the rain

art center
in the middle of industry
artists

artist's total wealth
in his unsold paintings
poverty

art show
pain of false hope in all
the paint

covered with pollen
looking deep into a flower
camera lens

drawing
with my hand goes
this fly

holding the day
between my hands
the new clay bowl

in the photo
it leans to the north
grandpa's ice house

made of sky
the blue pencil
drawing clouds

photographing
a boring scene just because
perfect clouds

sumi sketch
the ink shine fades
into flute notes

sunshine
painting the beach
just as it is

in the picture
enough spring water
for my brush

the potter
gives the bowl the shape
of her hand

the prize
in the art show
not getting it

unfurling black
petals to the flower light
camera shutter

vacation students
learning in the art gallery
anatomy

waterfall painting
dripping enough water
to tint the rock

worn down
the view so oft photographed
from this rock

at the beach
a little cloud
as a child runs before
the lowering sun

a nap
in the sweet smell
of straw hat

after he passed
still wearing the smile
he gave me

after the holiday
tracks on the beach
one sandal

asleep on the sand
the smell of the sea
in my hand

at the elbow
of the bathing beauty
her first wrinkles

beach breakfast
at-home foods taste
of the sea

beach clock
the tide-soaked jeans
slowly dry

beach clock
the sunburn begins
to sting

beachcomber
collecting early morning
in shells

beach cosmetic
suntan lotion with sand
and ants

beach meditation
alone and then joined
by the sun

beach meditation
a boat load of fisher guys
turns away

beach narrowed
by afternoon high tide
every one sleeps

beach path
drawn on a map
too short

beach picnic
between bites
haiku – sand

beach picnic
the strong wind gets
most of it

boogie boards
when one falls into
surf sounds

bridge shadow
our picnic area
slides east

child-like
her sand castles where
he wants her

circling around
the beach umbrella
the sun and its shade

divorcee's beach date
as if the little kids behind
are not hers

end of the day
everything sticks
to suntan lotion

gifts
for borrowing her beach
coffee and cake
                    -for Pamela Nelson

hello to the sea
and already my pockets
full of shells

high tide
the cliff shadow
disappears

hour by hour
the blanket covered
with drifting sand

late summer
alone on the beach
with only tracks

leaving the book
her bare legs read
the waves

lovers' sandcastle
the little waves of sunset
go around it

lovers' sandcastle
how smooth the beach
by nightfall

low tide
2 beer bellies in a boat
take her for a ride

lying on the beach
with the voices of seals
people talk

memory
in my shoulder afternoon
sunburn

mother and daughter
walking down the beach with
father and son

palm reading
in rows of darkness
gritty sand

people shrinking
by the sea huge rocks
seen from the beach

picking up shells
ah! there's an old one
moon in a tide pool

sand castle
joyous little boys play
king of the hill

shipping lanes
from rock to rock
goes the hour

sitting here
the far sea horizon comes
to each lap

sleeping soundly
suddenly surrounded
by sea

swallowtail
a nickname for the guy
who likes to do it

smearing
shade on her nose
sun lotion

smelling of fish
two men sit and talk
on the beach

spread-eagled
on the beach beside her
osprey shadow

sudden laughter
sea water whacks the rock
to see the tourists run

the colors
wading in tide pools
a part of her

the day and I
going to the beach
without tracks

the high tide
in wet blue jeans
not yet gone

tides of people
the pull of the sea
on a summer day

tired picnic
how to eat lying down
in sandy wind

voices
the beach path brings
visitors

walking away
the roar of the sea
still in my bones

warmer winds
the whole family comes
to the beach

white shoes
worn by city kids
tide pool green

boats

a cracked canoe
floating on the river
all my years

a crown
for the ancestors in stone
the flower boat

adorned with flowers
the boat of blossoming
comes ashore

afternoon
taking the river home
in poems

along this path
a boat was borne
with song

at ease
crossing over huge rocks
clouds – kayaks

Big River
looks even larger
in a boat

blowing cornmeal
and a cloud of pollen
blessing the boat

breath of the sea
in the buoy bell
a warning voice

canoe silence
floating down the river
something silk

dark seas
the flower boat floats
alight

down river
the trip takes
half the time

evening chain
holding the boat fast
to the buoy

flower boat
white clouds sail
above the sea

flower stems
curving the boat
into the sea

from boat to boat
our off-key singing echoes
over the river

from rock to rock
the fishing boat goes
home

from the dream
of rowing the river
blisters
                    -for Clemens

high and dry
the boat lowers my butt
into deep water

left right
no one knows where
the canoe goes

lying in shadow
yet able to see
the boat spirits

raised and lowered
against something soft
boat bow

rented canoe
suddenly Indian life
very risky

river smell
inside the kayak
after the portage

sailor's wife
the twinkle in her eye
from the sunlit sea

shaped by hands
the ship of flower shapes
sails with spirits

summer dusk
in the silence of a fishing boat
its lantern

the river narrows
around the canoe
more wind

tied to the boat
the beauty of flowers
our invisible souls

tipping the canoe
every wave comes in
as passenger

tipping the canoe
every wave comes in
for the ride

to go somewhere
waves slapping the sides
of a boat

two women
floating on the river
their stories

waterproof
an afternoon of haiku
dropped in the river

water wobble
back on land we can
hardly walk

willow wand boat
the sea comes and goes
in it

camping

campfire
in a grove of trees
night theater

campfire
in the dark woods
eyes

cold leaving
two on the gravel bank
a vitamin D rest
-thanks to Harmony

coming nearer
a shift of embers
darkness

family picnic
taking one back to childhood
summer breezes

Fort Ross
defending nature
with a park

ice water
home from camping
the luxury again

it feels illicit
sleeping so close to nature
camping in the wilds

legs of a bear
the seedling pines have grown
in the darkness

lost in the woods
the cold wind of the sea
directs the darkness

picnic ground
covered with acorns
candy wrappers

on a camping trip
lost in the mountains
finding autumn

children

anglers
the oldest child catches
the first fish

camp kids
toasting marshmallows
their eyes melt

catching the ball
his hands pulled upward
where it is

circle of new grass
the kid's eyes when he hears
the space ship landed here

dirt on her face
the model child
cuter

divorce
brings another child home
mosquitoes on the screen

fifteen
the scrape of a razor
music to his ears

filled with kids
how can one say
the tree is old

lost child
the name of a designer
on his chest

night tide
children's tracks erased
by their leaving

professional papa
with a power company's crane
hanging the kid's swing

single mom
trying to make a man
out of her thin son

sun-warmed skin
the smell of childhood
again on an old woman

summer baby
finally one that sleeps
through the night

chores

a familiar face
in the courthouse
a copy machine

doing dishes
resentment takes me back
to mother's kitchen

folding underwear
a hammock swings between
fig trees

grinding stone
bright with woman spirits
after the rain

hills added to
a mountain of laundry
shells and sand

jury assembly
so many people
so many minds

pegging the wash
a rapping on the clothes pole
by a woodpecker

outdoor shower
surrounded by the flowers
of sunlit water

scorching sun
mom decides it is too hot
to iron clothes

the hum of voices
waiting in the waiting room
increasing warmth

cleaning

after my shower
in the canyon
more rain

a new flower
the humming bird watches
the guy pee

artist housekeeper
the cleanest spots
are paintings

clean hair
and the ocean is calm
Saturday

house clean
the day begins with
morning calm

roadside privy
a big puddle by the door
after the rain

summer light
a woman's song pours out
with bath water

under the bush
the dark shadows
of pee places

clothes and adornment

buxom dame
words on her t-shirt
HONEY WELL

coolness of a fan
sticks and white paper
of a snowy scene

curls in my hair
from the new leaf hat
worms

costumed
her face rapt
in old music

drying on the porch
freshly washed sweaters
far away sheep

first day of summer
the longest pair of pants
cut off

high heels
within a city block
seasick

high top
black tennis shoes
in Point Arena

his jacket too short
the organ grinder's monkey
bends to get the coin

in my ear
abalone earrings
sea sounds

if the wind wants it
letting my hat fly
to the rocks below

in the cold
hugging myself with
jacket sleeves

knowing no shame
wind blows up the dress
of the fat lady

low-tide weather
salt-stained trouser legs
sandy pockets of air

moon light
filling our shoes
for a walk

my face
under a hat
my dad

same style
the blue dress worn more
than the black

slipping off
his sport jacket
wedding band

sun hats
straw-filled radiance
halos

the hot lady's
only ornaments
beads of sweat

the heat
unbuttoning his shirt
he's even hotter

the old guy
in his new jeans
a big belly

the oldest costumes
a woman carries a child
on her hip

walking away the cold
abandoned in the next cove
a sweatshirt

watered silk
bright surf catches
her pant leg

wrinkles
in her t-shirt
giggles

dreaming
an open window
the sea and I share
this bed

high tide nap
waiting for the water
to wake me

moonset
in the plop of waves
sleep

napping
in an afternoon sky
all the clouds

new bedspread
from Portugal becomes
a traveler

river rock walls
dreaming in this house
flows in all seasons

ripples
on calm waters
sailors' dreams

sea cottage
in the pile of pillows
fog smell

sea light
getting into bed
before it goes

unable to sleep
the neighbor who waters
his lawn at night

eating and drinking
a glass of water
in me another
clear thought

all day the star
light mints in her
diet

a soup smell
in picnic sandwiches
bay leaves

another piece of chocolate
quick before it expires
in two years

eating seaweed
forgetting to wash off the sand
our giggles

evening
the last wine glass
holds the light

future seasons
the glass waiting to be filled
with wine days

heat wave
peeling eggs for a salad
naked

iced tea
end of the afternoon
in the slurpy sound

iced tea
so much pleasure
with no calories

just now
with the incoming tide
supper time

lunch
the forgotten knife
becomes a finger

making iced tea
in the same pitcher
all the hot days

mountain tasting
granite stone water
in a tin cup

peeling pears
the family gathers
as fruit salad

pine fire smoke
the delight in someone else's
breakfast

on a journey
the foods from home
never taste right

Sagami Bay
in my tea bowl
the art of Japan

salt water taffy
no salt or water
sugar-free

selling cider
by the fruit stand
restrooms

singing
for our dinner
the wind

sunshine on roses
selling the salesman
a jar of honey

the dark beacon
on the summer porch
sun-tea

the fallen tree
staying in the park
a picnic table

the shape
before the darkness
wine glass light

wine glass
half full and overflowing
with jazz

with coffee
the sun breaks through
the fog

vegetarians
watching the cat eat
a still-warm bird

vegetarian
dragons watching her eat
at the Thai diner

vegetarian
onion-mustard sandwich
from student days

entertainments
a coffee grinder
the mulatto stripper
smells good

afternoon TV
watching the fog drift
over the bay

bumping and floating
the breath of someone else
in a balloon

collecting people
shade of the apple tree
dulcimer music

competition won
for the best perfume bottle
rose water

deep cough
the unseen guy
in the balcony

dimples in a spa
the fat lady and
the rain

giant redwoods
here the men carry
long guns

hammock view
swinging back and forth
the sea and me

history lives
with the oldest tune
people clapping

marathon winners
warming the sun
with their hands

local movie goers
side by side with New Yorkers
at the Met

rained out
the yard sale upgrades
to the garage

rained out ballgame
adults too play
trivial pursuit

rubberstamp show
bargain hunters pushed
out of shape

silence
faces at the party
in a mirror

still young
auntie knows how to make
hollyhock dolls

traffic
by my hammock
ships - gophers

the lights dim
we move together
on the screen

the stolen rope
how high we get
swinging

the way the day goes
an invitation to the park
as a folded paper boat

waiting
for the movie to start
our many lives

water to water
in the hot tub two persons
as it rains

yard sale weather
to think someone wore this
last winter

fireworks
after the fireworks
only Venus and the bell buoy
still shine

another star
still no fireworks
boom!

before the fireworks
car lights curve on the hills
on the way to town

before the fireworks
in the new moon's darkness
sparkles

boom
before the fireworks
a door slams

cold ocean wind
fireworks boom
even louder

colored wind
with a whoosh exploding
fireworks

couples
huddle under blankets
fireworks

drought over
the fireworks hidden
by trees

each year
lower on the neighbor's tree
fireworks

fireworks
afterwards the stars too
fall into the sea

fireworks
at dusk the biggest light
in the smoke

fireworks
before it gets dark enough
a foreign language

fireworks
crystal colors
of salt wind

fire works
in the summer night
red green and blue

fireworks
silently coming into view
a star

fireworks
slowly exploding
stars

fireworks
suddenly the ocean wind
is warmer

from the waves
waiting for fireworks
spindrift

golden
the first arch of fireworks
the setting moon

illegal
yet celebrating independence
fire crackers

in our laps
the small town enjoys
fireworks

in the cove
jellyfish float below
fireworks

late holiday
fireworks still reflected
in the water

light flowers
bloom and boom
fireworks

lighthouse beam
searching the coast
for the fireworks

light lingers
it too is waiting for
fireworks

light show
brighter than fireworks
cars leaving town

moonset
the first fireworks
golden

mouth closed
fireworks explode over
the estuary

nautical twilight
the day extended by waiting
for the fireworks

nautical twilight
too bright still
for fireworks

neon colored creatures
floating above the sea
fireworks

out over the sea
an audience of boats
for fireworks

red and green
on watermelon rinds
fireworks

sky dark
still the glow of fireworks
in our eyes

there
between the tree limbs
a sparkle

the way home
after the fireworks
Venus over the sea

the smallest town
has with its rich folks
more fireworks

wearing a halo
then the child's sparkler
goes dark

waiting for fireworks
the first spray of colors
in the sunset

waiting for the Fourth
we stare at a sunset
not yet dark

waiting with giggles
and then the silence
of fireworks

wave upon wave
waiting for fireworks
another wave

fishing
cast into the trees
sun from the stream
lost lures

fighting the hook
the fish jumps into
a sea of clouds

fish
climbing the hill with
two tired men

fisherman
evening goes with him
into the boat house

fly fishing
the hook catches him
right in front

still flying
the feather tied
to a lure

furniture

cabin fever
the bedside table is
a kitchen chair

faded brown cover
farts still shaped by
the old chair

hands
sweeping away the day
the clock

high winds
on the balcony a chair
rocks itself

how hot
the sound of a fridge
running fast

squeak squeak
even the porch swing
seems to gossip

in its arms
my favorite chair bids me
fare thee well

the moon
bends down to set afire
a mirror

the tall thin woman
elegant in the rattan chair
her coolness

gardening

dry thunder
in the parched garden
the thudding hoe

over-grown
sun and shadow share
garden quiet

setting bean poles
a tendril stays curled
around my finger

guests

a fan opens
the bones of fingers
high five

already late
the guests leave us alone
to enjoy the view

company coming
mist shapes upon the sea
before it rains

going yet staying
the summer vacation
guests

how to tell
the . . . guy his tires
are. . . too

rare beach rocks
sea-worn but sharp
famous people

summer guests
it seems my job to make sure
the weather is nice

Sunday visitors
in the afternoon I receive
a few poems

the deep days
in the beginning of summer
our friendship

visitors coming
where to hide
our bad habits

harbors
facing the harbor
a new moon too
watches fireworks

harbor lights
even the stars smell
of fish

harbor smells
tangled on the pier
ropes

heavy rain
on the dock a fisherman's net
is full

in the harbor
the sailboat enters
evening calm

in the river
no fear of the fishers' songs
a tree as rod

rising and falling
every-sized boat
in the bay

waterfront bar
none of the glasses filled
with water

health issues
a fart
the wordless goodbye
to my appendix

after the accident
in traditional melodies
all the pain

after the divorce
seeing how a leaf heals
where the worm was

a white cane
listening to the sidewalk
go up and down

also gray on top
my one-legged friend is more
than a cane

among pines
supported by green
I cast off my cane

between showers
my hospital roomie wets
her bed

closing my eyes
to dish-washing noises
summer illness

daily medicine
air hanging over rocks
at low tide

for the fetus
the white rose bud
damaged by rain

get-well cards
limp in the morning fog
I sleep again

handicapped
the tense voice saying
please and *thank-you*

home from the hospital
the pain still in the high notes
shakuhachi

if you could pick
the best illness to have
appendicitis

numbing
the hours
morphine

old and lame
the wise woman knows best
the grace of dancing

paperwork
for my discharge
the sun

recovery
tubes and stitches
wired

recovery room
voices calling me back
to myself my pain

recuperating
the quiet sea sound
at ebb tide

spilled pop
his one crisis
in ER

so many cupboards
in which one is kept
a bottle of health

summer thinness
my white leg freed
from the cast

the body cut open
flowers enter in their
own red wounds

the joy
in each new room
closer to surgery

a whiny groaner
with no symptoms
goes home last

vertical
or horizontal
a slit decision

waiting
for hospital discharge
showers

weaving voices
the sway of gurneys
in ER

heating
a guest's rude word
in the summer fireplace
drifting soot

all night
the roar of the river
the gas heater

illegal campfire
6 men and a truck
and a bill to match

leaving home
smoke from the chimney
in weak sunlight

still life
fresh roses on the stove
for painting

sunset
a fire in the sea cave
burns the poems

hiking
a summer hike
in mountain shadows
finding autumn

up the mountain
the moon whiter
with each step

first sweat
at the *no admittance* sign
climbing the fence

low tide walk ends
at the edge of the bay
blue skies

no-parking signs
at the head of the trail
for hikers

not so clear
the puddle jumped
with a misstep

restored
the finger-wide waterfall fills
my summer hat

storm waves
climbing higher on the cliff
the hikers

hitch-hiking
is that my ride
coming down the road?
only canyon wind

housing
this house
with river rock walls
flows in itself

in this house
river rock walls dream
a stony silence

a fence or wall
I sleep inside the wood
of unbudded flowers

a home
the invisible heart of sticks
shells and bones

all those houses
all those heads
each another world

back woods cabin
a candle moves shadows
from here to there

buying a house
the trees old enough to swing
a hammock

ceiling beam
the first flute notes
in the wood

cease-fire
a flight of stairs
going nowhere

climbing the stairs
a woman's shrill laugh
over my head

cloak room
among lost coats
a bib

coming into
the cool darkened room
sunglasses for my body

condemned
million dollar homes
sea sides slipping

even before cut
the stand of trees
a fence

forest cabin
mountain stillness
thickens the walls

going to bed
naked
Venus in the window

growing in rock
another piece of drift wood
added to the shelter

hermits
buying a new house
on the corner

housewarming
under a cathedral ceiling
all of us saints

in the eaves
of the summer house
swallows' nest

light
boxed out with cedar wood
a new house

mountain wind
it stretches me out
on a sunny porch

nameless
clusters of summer homes
bigger than towns

neighbor's house
a sneeze echoes
in emptiness

neighbors' houses
where they stay home
we move on

no trespassing sign
it only keeps others out
where our eyes go

Odd Fellows Hall
from red hot jazz
to firetrap

old wrinkled arms
embracing us again
wood-grain walls

open to all
on the beach a shelter
for the spirits

paintings
the shine of a mind
on the walls

rain storm ends
my powerless room
grows lighter

rough shed
light on the walls
paintings

remnants of fog
the things people leave
in the rental house

sea breeze
sun-warmed it stays
on the porch

seaside cottage
the smell of towels
ebb tide

vacation houses
the sea shining with
sun pennies

shutters closed
that is not how I remember
the summer cabin

stone crop
the realtor earns more
on seaside houses

Sunday church
on the sunny porch
me and a sparrow

tenement housing
a box of broken glass
spray-painted

the dark beacon
on the summer porch
sun-tea

the redwood forest
in French window panes
eye-sized bits

thickening clouds
the happy campers crowd
in one motel

Timber Cove
the houses all built
of wood

unfinished house
already a sunset view
in its window

waiting for someone
a vacant house overlooking
the sea

music
ancients listen
to the flute concert
stone ears

banjo player
the vibes come through
the bench we share

bare feet
raising dust in time
with old music

bell silence
hanging before the flute
in-taken breath

between his lips
the bamboo flute
becomes a song

between his fingers
and the baby grand piano
the music

blue lights
the slow rhythms
of low notes

chills
of late afternoon
guitar prayers

disco ball
mirrors spinning
ragas

drum dance
done without sticks
a joyous kid

every one chatting
he hammers the dulcimer
for the green apples

fingers flying
over black and white keys
the blue lights

first ipod
the background music
of waves

fitting together
shade under an apple tree
banjo music

flute concert
the old man's fingers
play along

flute music
under the spell
the pen stops

flute notes
the empty shoes
are all open

heat
in the room
wine smell

heartfelt
the drummer keeping time
with his foot

heart strings
in the wooden flute
a quivering

lacking a drum
heart and fingers beat
a rib-laced hollow

in and out
the music breathes
for the harmonica

in suits and ties
their jazz comes straight
from the seventies

jazz program
all the listeners
are white

moving
during the loud notes
the chair squeaks

no song
the flute just
breathes

overflowing
the flute empties
its notes

pelvic thrusts
Mississippi river mud
on their minds

purple haze
garlic breath played
on a flute

raga
spaces in the spinning
gone

saxophone
the beginning of headache
squawks

shoe string handle
the guitar case holds
two coins

sign language
instruments completing
a crescendo

spinning
raga colors
disco mirror

staring
back in time
old melodies

stilled flute
music familiar
to the trees

sun down
sliding between redwoods
flute notes

tension
between the flute notes
attention

the call
of her cleavage
first notes

the prayer begins
with indrawn breath
a silent flute

touching holes
the flute master teaches
singing

twinkling
in the vibraphone
ringing tones

outdoor concerts
adagio
the caution tape
quivers

after intermission
the gentle beginning
of dove calls

after the concert
my souvenir is the tune
I can hum

applause
the music belongs
to the stars

applause
the music returns to
the performers

ancient listening
to the flute concert
stones

a scenic spot
the flute master shines
above the sea

bells
neighbors play horseshoes
during the house concert

between tall trees
the lowest flute note
at sunset

between notes
the loss of control
by a waterfall

call of the flute
answer of drums
among redwoods

classical music
ending the concert
a river's sound

concert
the squealing women hug
long-lost friends

concert talk
shiny shoes against
the stones

dancing
from cloud to trees
island drums

death songs
the cactus bends
a spent flower

drumming
the scrunch of gravel
by late-comers

drum music
written in the clouds
white and blue

dusty path
coming to the concert
in sandals

eight performers
twenty instruments
singing

everyone
dressed up
casual

far from home
players and instruments
welcome

fledglings
launched from a branch
flute notes

flute concert
in the surf sea stones
move at sunset

flute concert
coming through the screen
ant feet

flute concert
speaking Japanese fluently
the shakuhachi

flute lullaby
song birds going
to sleep

fresh tonight
those old songs
sung again

glass beads
the notes of the concert
shining sound

good-byes
sparking in the parking lot
dim flashlights

harmonizing
before the concert
perfumes

history
in the wine glass
all that jazz

home again
after the concert the music
back in the stars

in his arms
the curve of the drum's
sound

intermission chatter
shiny shoes shuffle
in the gravel

intermission
crowds around tables
of food & CDs

intermission
the modern music turns
to chatter

intermission
a woman tips her head
to drink

in the dark
music for each alone
togetherness

island fishermen
singing with foreigners
learning to clap

island frugality
two musicians on
one drum

late comer
to the outdoor concert
the neighbor's dog

later
coming to the concert
moths

mating dance
the flute concert comes
to an end

mic hum
the flute master
takes note

modern music
another layer of flagstone
crumbles

modern music
audience noise
absorbed

modern music
a flock of dragonflies
overhead

modern music concert
construction zone surrounded
by caution tape

morning after
still humming the tune
How High the Moon

music rocking
the composer's granddaughter
her baby

nearly empty
the wine glass overflows
with jazz

night
flute tuned
breath

notes
coming together
in smiles

ocean waves
on the darkening shore
flute notes

on a stage
the beat of the city
in our feet

on the porch
pairs of shoes and I listen
to the concert

outdoors
the music
cool

outdoors
the music sounds
free

outdoor concert
the flute master warms
my ears

outdoor concert
smoke from a neighbor's cigar
comes also

outdoor flute concert
above the rustic village
campfire smoke

outdoor flute concert
the neighbors play badminton
with the notes

redwood needles
on the path to the concert
many voices

shakuhachi
calling through the trees
with two notes

sold out
the concert
even hotter

strange smell
listening to outdoor music
an unseen animal

sunset
flute called with gold
radiance

sunset concert
between the trees
wood smoke

the finale
at the last note
eight smiles

the shore recedes
into the stone of a flute's
notes

the way they walk
through the parking lot
no longer strangers

the woods
flute tuned
with wind

time
tying the jazz
into a group

times
between the notes
a jazz beat

wind sighs
redwoods applaud
shakuhachi player

without sticks
the performers drumming
on their thighs

poetry reading

blue eyes
above the poetry
FOOF logo

faded blossoms
a young poet finds his mentor
wears a leg brace

free to all
25 listeners
passion

gripping the neck
of his guitar tighter
his poetry worsens

moaning
is it the poetry
or the jazz

old lady voice
high above the sax
D.H. Lawrence

poetry reading
all the women bring
their boobs

swept along
poems applauded at a reading
by more wind

the thirty ideas
of the beat poets
autistic audience

the well dry
jazz & poetry changes
the wine

undercurrents
beneath the jazz noise
broken poems

play
humming along
with the Russian Choir
cold war forgotten

left from
the flight of gulls
kites

pulling and tugging
when the kite string goes slack
room to rise

12 years old
and as tall as Dad
on his new stilts

rented house sequence

sunset
the rented house reverts
to its owners

quarter moon
time to leave
the rented house

who will be your eyes
house, when all the blinds
are shut?

who will be your breath
house, when only spiders
swing from the ceiling?

will your floors ache
for the tread of feet
or just groan?

who will offer up
smells of roast beef and pies
damp mold?

the cold hearth
how will it be without warmth
of a grateful heart?

when birds sing
how can you, house
fill the feeder?

do you think, house
your crooked weather vane
can guide passing whales?

without my hands
to wave to northbound geese
house, will you notice?

who tints the sea blue
if my eyes aren't here
on sunny days?

who sings praises
to you in the evening
without my haiku?

who fills the knotholes
with music for you, house?
my flute goes with me

who holds up the roof
if my prayers are not
in your ridgepoles

at sunset
who remembers the colors
in your glass?

nights when the cold roar
of the sea fills the rooms
house, will you shiver?

where will stars sleep
house, when no eye opens
in the darkness?

who will listen to
the grey-brown of your cedar
speaking to the deer?

at daybreak
who touches the perfect dew
on your porch?

at noon
who rings the buoy bell
as delight with joy?

house, will you blow
away without the pretty stones
I bring from the beach?

who will bring flowers
for your tables
even in winter?

in a dusty pile
surely the sea shells
will pale and fade

without me, house
you'll have only visiting mice
and sow bugs

how will we live
without each other
as our houses?

star gazing
coming inside
after star gazing
my glow

our galaxy
in a folding chair
a star gazer

swimming
a cloud floating
in August's slow river
my jade body

after a swim
the skin dries on
a new person

afternoon cloud
the pee in me goes into
the sea

after the swim
the ocean bluer
with cold

blue sky and sea
swimming colors
on blue skin

cold water
warming itself
on my thigh

hardly Aphrodite
but I have been swimming
in the sea

my best dress
lying in the summer river
naked

my wealth
while lying naked in the river
sun pennies

naked in the stream
all my hungers filled
by sun sparkles

only smiles
my nakedness in the river
wrinkled

river swim
waves in my hair
newly cut

standing still
you know a swimmer
is taking a pee

swimming
the bull kelp gives me
a water toy

the ocean
swimming in
me in it

the old koan
what was I before I was born
naked in a summer river

wading in deeper
a sea of the born and unborn
touches my thigh

tea ceremony
after the tea
the giggling
for photos

bringing the tea
a scroll on the wall
spells coolness

cleansing
the tea utensils
our hearts

come & get it
service at the rustics'
tea ceremony

four hours
the serenity of
the thin tea

fushin hana
mysteriously the ceremony
and flowers open

summer day
the coolness
in the tea

tea ceremony
even Western guests seem
Japanese

tea ceremony
eyes caressing
the utensils

tea ceremony
only the Japanese dare
to take photos

the chattering
of camera shutters
thin tea

unwavering
the hand holding the ladle
the steam

transportation
180 degree curve
again we are headed
home

$2.65 a gallon
the bargain gas takes us
to the wedding

airport nerves
even in the florist shop
buds closed tight

a pit stop
all the new smells
back in the car

carsick
the bag of dirty laundry
overflows

drawing a line
straight over the sea
a sailing ship

gas pumps
at the pit stop
wind chimes

holiday cruise ship
without a sound party lights
pass me by

fellow traveler
one thumb hitch-hiking
the other in a book

flying high
on a flight of stairs
airport

flying too low
the propeller's shape
of infinity

for the flight
inviting the angels
to fly along

for the wedding
a coach and four
the bit so shiny

guiding us
a hastily picked flower
on the dash

Highway One
a cow path a 100 years later
still trod by cattle

limp with waiting
in the windless sun
sails

living history day
the helicopter circles
the ancient schooner

ocean liner
a darker hue in the blues
of sea and sky

at road markers
conversation changes
the subject

road slippage
driving faster over
the cave in

seaside
watching my neighbor go by
in his boat

sawmill town
logging trucks we've followed
now we meet

shiny car antenna
on the weather report
a glimpse of sun

slat fence
one part grows taller
as the ship comes

spangled seas
surrounded by darkness
the cruise ship

summer
the hot sound of passing
cars

traffic jam
a free-flowing river
under the bridge

wind
filling our eyes
with sails

vacation
a blur of kites
driving too fast
by the tourist trap

a boy's view
of the bay from the bridge
toy sailboats

back home
the family again
looks familiar

back to work
it must have melted
my summer vacation

chapped skin
leaving in a rented room
bits of me

far from home
not knowing the place
where the sun rises

holiday over
crowds on the highway
overcast skies clear

hot dry country
all the skinny women
dried to leather

ignoring tourists
whales dive and the shadows
swing the hammock

left and right
the moon bounces over
a mountain road

migrating whales
my packed suitcase
looks pregnant

mountain pass
we too are stopped
by the view

mein deutsch
ist ein bischen komisch
smiles are international

my sea view
sun sparkles as
neighbors

open road
spots of sun
on the map

on vacation
the thin woman wears
a man's shirt

packing it in
the over-filled suitcase
the too-small bikini

remote coast
in a general store
a Paris doll

sun burnt
the old guy seems
much younger

stiff and sore
too tired to feel
the sunburn

sunrise
one and a half hours
from home

sunset
arriving in Point Arena
the beat generation

steel fountain
the base covered with copper
coins

the altar
packed and ready to fly
all the saints

tourism down 50%
the Golden Gate Bridge
a rusty orange

trade winds
the outdoor vendor
offers to barter

traveling
the waves closer
than ever before

12 hours on the road
the same quarter moon
over the canyon

tourist shop
over the sound of crashing
waves
buy me! – buy me!

tourist shop
nothing anyone needs
for sale

tourist town
the resident artist carries
a parasol

Twin Rocks
the community has
two churches

underground
at the hot spring inn
potatoes

village sunshine
between the redwoods
visitors' awe

we end up
looking for the winery
Soda Springs

with the redwoods
taking a trip to China
in Gualala

wrong turn
in a foreign country
darkness overtakes us

women
a diamond
glistening on her finger
a teardrop

a life together
two women stand barefoot
in the river

women talking
in the smallest room
thin smell of blood

writing and reading
again our goddess
holds aloft the light
of postage stamps

golden evening
writing haiku permits me
to stare at the sea

Hawaiian haiku
the ukulele song
5-7-5

marking the book
an afternoon breeze
and sand

mountain skyline
and puffs of cloud
a torn envelope

on the beach
grinding my ink
with sand

part ink
on sea sand paper
the day

proof reading
the first mark
chocolate

reading aloud
Chinese poetry
coolness

sea stone
filling the hole
with ink

sea-written poem
new in my pocket
wave wet

shape changing
the words in a book
under dappled sun

summer reading
the murder mystery
gives me chills

summer reading
wind turns the pages
drops in a leaf

the heat
to pull around oneself
the text of a haiku

the pen scribbles
driving by the history
of small towns

the poem written
on transparent paper
foggy morning

the shape of poems
when light shines through
sounds

thin ink on
paper white of a snowy scene
coolness of a fan

unable to speak
handwriting fills the postcard
from edge to edge

work

resting
beside the old folks
a young tern

spirit work
crunching words
in the computer

uprooted
swaying in the kelp beds
the floundered boat

weaver woman
the calluses on her feet
thumbs

SUMMER Animals

ants

ants
the kitchen never has
just one

bark color
climbing the tree
with the ant

borrowed legs
one ant can't move
the large leaf

curious
no one reads my poems
except this ant

high tide
on the island
ants and me

memorial service
among the uninvited guests
ants

praying mantis
its wish is eaten
by the ants

sex call
to all beach ants
suntan lotion

sparks of life
burn brighter with the heat
ants

bees

a golden ray
among the low blue flowers
a bumble bee

borage
bringing bees to the end
of the path

cool morning
the bee comes inside
the flower I picked

exciting the air
between flowers
bee lines

house arrest
the hornets' nest
by the back door

ochre stripes
holes in the ground where
bumble bees enter

the bee and I
face to face
in a flower

birds

a bird calls
morning light comes
to the island

a bird vanishes
the summer day goes
without it

a vanishing bird
the summer day
goes with it

afternoon stillness
only the whir of wings
stirs the air

air currents
twisting the shadows
of a bird

a softer gold
in the afternoon's heat
call of mourning doves

balance act
waiting for the train
pigeons on a wire

before sleeping
the smallest bird chirps
with my prayer

bilingual
giving the hawk
a German name

bird bath
with a flapping of wings
it becomes a shower

bird calls
the sea comes ashore
as a plea

bird nerves
electricity of the air
moves feathers

birds
filled with air
fly into it

blue skies
a darkness flies from the tree
in birds

country lodging
all the beggars are
birds and squirrels

dawn song
the sky lightened
by bluebirds

darkness
falling off the cliff
bird shadow

escaping
the overcast sky
bird song

faces
on the rock changing
birds

from tree to tree
the first birds fly
into the moon

fusion jazz
with the shakuhachi
call of a quail

into the sunlight
the kingfisher brings his blue
coolness

invited by larks
to the top of the hill
a great idea

kelp island
more each day with
the egrets' arrival

lifting off the rock
that dark pinnacle
a bird

memorial service
among the uninvited guests
vultures

morning moon
in its slenderness
a peeping bird

midnight
singing stolen songs
the mockingbird

mountains
folding into a valley
bird wings

partly cloudy skies
the sunshine comes
with birdsong

roadside rest
trees around parked cars
filled with birds

soaring
the bird out flies
its name

summer appears
on the lawn young birds
seem unsure

summer nights
in the crooked birdhouse
our bats

thoughts flying
in delightful excitement
following a bird

thunder nearby
where finches disappear
ripples in the birdbath

topsail island
the rocks whitened
by nesting birds

tourists
in the seaside resort
grackles and starlings

ups and downs
floating birds secure
on a stormy sea

vacation
learning from the dove
its other voices

weaving the river
the water ouzel and
its song

wren song
filling my canteen
at the spring

bugs

from the book
"How to Tie Flies"
a silverfish

giving in to the heat
the drone of some bug's
mid-day nap

mayonnaise jar
with wisps of grass
firefly lantern

orange and red
from hill to hill changes
in ladybug colors

picnic food
the family on the patio
eaten by bugs

still black
the beetle crawling on a red
Indian paintbrush

such a short night
not one insect sleeps
in my wakefulness

sucking juices
from rose buds
stink bugs

uninvited guests
the house sells for less
with termites

walking the stream
on spots of sunlight
the water beetle

butterflies

a butterfly pauses
in the mystery of each other
we gaze

art show activity
a butterfly flits from flower
to flower

blessing the children
in the outdoor church
a butterfly

butterflies
moving over her bare back
bones

butterflies
skipping the stone that cross
the brook

butterfly wings
with a slow flapping
summer waves

California sisters
the butterfly goes with me
over the bridge

caught
the pattern of wings
in the butterfly net

deer tracks
from a patch of wildflowers
a butterfly

in Mariposa
greetings and blessings
from butterflies

into the sun
a butterfly's passing
the end of summer

still pond
the butterfly's shadow floats
over rocks

sunny day
the sky yellow
with butterflies

caterpillars

caterpillars
related to the cat
only by play

those fabled worms
known and yet unknown
made of silk

saving a tree
the caterpillar wants
to live also

such heat
caterpillars cool off
on cucumbers

cats

a cat's affection
in a flash of lightning
a change of heart

cat fight
the skinny feral one
howls the loudest

cat owner
burying on the beach
dog poop

curled up asleep
the cat after eating
a snake

dog days
the howling in this house
both cats

eclipse
the cat eats dog food
without noticing

evening fog
the feral cat is the same
color

extra clothes
and the cat's big eyes
into the suitcase

friends again
two cats with a window
between them

herb patch
the oldest cat
in the sage

home again
the cat cries
our cries

looking for a cat
I found the night full
of lost things

moon meditation
the cat brings to the cushion
a favorite toy

nights longer
the stray cat's tail
over his feet

not yet human
the nurse asking if
I am a cat person

only a cat
staring at the spot where
the moon rises

playing with the cat
the wise sparrow
just out of reach

rolling sunshine
the ginger cat nabs
the catnip toy

thunder
the white cat jumps down
from the windowsill

waiting for fireworks
the cat walks back and forth
under my hand

chickens

bones of a chicken
one dinner for a gull
after ours

bride's cookout
the rich in-laws eat chicken
with knife and fork

chicken bones
the gull's hoarse cry
after our picnic

into the air
by the kite shop
a rooster crows

sunshine
in the hen's beak
a voice of eggs

chipmunks

beach picnic
crumbling from the cliffs
chipmunks

moving sunshine
in and out of shadow
chipmunks

cicada

cicada prayers
even louder in the heat
clacking beads

golden light
silence in a cicada
the husk

mom dying
waiting for the cry
of a cicada

sound of the sea
here in the mountains
cicada surf

the cicada
drumming to the stars
all is still

to be as faithful
to my prayers as cicadas
the heat

cormorants
lights
on the cormorant nesting place
the glisten of dung

ocean cool
evening in the voices
of cormorants

quarreling mothers
on bare sea rocks
cormorants

to porch cool
comes the voice of cormorants
exposed seaweeds

waterfall
over the basalt rocks
cormorant guano

cows
black and white
photo of Holsteins
and a heron

country girl
sleeping with her cow
before it is sold

calling the cows home
from the meadow comes
the moon

cows
standing on the road
even on signs

honking horns
to see the traffic the calf
turns its head

sea cliff meadows
heavy fog lifting
two. . . no, ten cows

crabs
alone on the beach
a hermit crab and I
dance for joy

beach shelter
made of driftwood for human
hermit crabs

crab boats
full even when empty
with fishy smells

delicate pastels
in the pain of a pinch
from a crab

high tide music
scurrying away
fiddler crabs

sea wall
safe in the cracks
soft-shelled crabs

deer

roses
disappearing
deer

seeing my cast
the deer lifts a foot
prances away

summer bracken
the shape of the spots
on the fawn

dogs

a dog
at the flute concert
panting

a new dog
the old couple younger
this afternoon

atonal music
time kept by the wagging
of a dog's tail

dog-eared
magazines
at the vet's

dog star
on my neighbor's back porch
all night the howling

end of summer
a stray dog follows
me home

fireworks
the old dog whimpers
like a puppy

ghost blue
on the pole a photo
of a lost dog

retrieved
in my rearview mirror
that yellow dog

dragons

dragon remnants
on the weathered rock
lizards

waterfall scroll
the green tea swallowed
with the dragon

dragonflies

dragonflies
stitching the air
sky blue

dragon fly wing
the blue sky back on
the veined leaf

drawn by the brush
the dragonfly points
the way

end of summer
even hotter by the breath
of dragonflies

fine art
in the city gallery
a dragonfly

lingering heat
red dragonflies mate
before the fall

looking for love
the dragonfly alights on
a red plastic straw

ducks

Bodega Bay
the ducks swim around
raindrop circles

feeding frenzy
ducks gather in the cove
high clouds

kayak floating
more at home on the water
ducks

sleeping ducks
rocked by the waves
of the summer moon

eagles

earth
higher than the hills
an eagle

going over
the mountain pass
with an eagle

farm animals

barnyard gate
the voice of the pig
in it

fish

a waxing moon
scales of a ling cod
fly from a knife

beside us
the canoe shape
of small fish

fish gather around
they allow me to lie down
in their creek

fish kisses
on this old body
once a fish

in the flame
the fish grows out
of glass

no TV
watching a fisherman
catch a blimey

splash
a fish opening a door
in the lake

sunlight
turning in the pond
goldfish

swimming
to keep me warm
minnows

tiny brown stone spots
along a blue-line stream
trout side

under the bridge
carp huddle
out of the rain

welcome
to the mountain stream
fish kisses

fleas and lice
as the topic turns
to the subject of lice
everyone scratches

fleas
only the neighbor's dog
has them

scratching fleas
the dog is distracted
by his dinner

flies
a fly
how can I kill the one
that licks my finger

beach meditation
complete with the cold
feet of flies

beach warmth
at high tide everything crawls
up on rocks

Buddhist vows
yet now and again she thinks
of the fly swatter

butterfly weeds
yet on me are sitting
only flies

drawing it
with my hand goes
this fly

glass puzzle
at the window the fly
and its buzzing

high noon
finally I am warm enough
for flies to sit on me

in seclusion
my only companion
a house fly

wind still
sparkles on the sea
many beach flies

frogs
frogs
sitting in the river
all of us

far from a pond
yet the tree has its own
frog

fat and ugly
the benefits of being
a toad

too hot
the motionless frog
in a sluggish pond

gnats
a cloud of gnats
rising into a swarm
of swallows

gnats
making a shape out
of a ray of sun

having lunch with me
very ripe peaches and
two gnats

passing clouds
the gnat dance goes on
in my hair

gulls
a fringe of light
lifted over the sea
a gull's wing

a sea gull
perched on a rock
my other self

campers gone
gulls take over
the fishing places

checking me out
for beach invasion
only young gulls

clearing fog
a flock of gulls sweep
to the lighthouse

gull flight
curved by the rocks
bird-shape

Jenner pit stop
the gulls laugh at
the shitty smell

last light
rising out of the cliff
seven gulls

laughter
as I put on my bathing suit
young gulls

left by the sea
a strange white shell
gull poop

long distance
the sea gull stands flat-footed
on a phone booth

low tide
leaving the beach
to a crying gull

playing river dare
gulls float backwards
to the sea

rounds
a sea gull circles
surf songs

starfish
all the days of its life
going into a gull

whirlwind rising
from the dead gull
a white feather

wind
waving waves
gulls

women
meeting on the beach
gull laughter

herons
a great heron
soaring above the water
this wobbly kayak

a lump in his throat
the great blue heron
nabs a gopher

as an apology
the heron unfolds
from a flight

feeding me
the heron leaves
a feather

meditation
minute by meter the heron
comes closer

spearing a herring
cocktail guests on the deck
the heron

to the island
where no one goes
a pair of herons

horses
the mountain ravine
has it own warm fragrance
horses and oaks

a horse whinnies
from inside the house a guy
blows his nose

hummingbird
a hummingbird
leaving wide spaces
in my hand

humming birds
a life of prayer and red flowers
invisible wings

my porch
hummingbirds fight each other
over the territory

sipping a soda
the hummingbird's tongue
a clear straw

sipping fuchsia
the hummingbird
closes his eyes

the flowered branch
one comes and goes as
a humming bird

jays
electrical wires
a blue line the sky
flight of a jay

high on tea
talking non-stop
blue jays

in morning quiet
the screech of jays
as the cat comes out

neighbors fighting
over nesting places
scrub jays

outdoor tea
the blue jay lunches
on spiders

summer grove
where a blue jay flies in
the coolness

the screech
that comes from his knees
blue jay's alarm

lizard
leaving the path
we bump into each other
the lizard and I

outdoors bath
watching through slatted eyes
the biggest lizard

rented cabin
the lizard hisses me
off his porch

sand dunes
scarred by the lizard
with his tracks

magpies
deep in the forest
an alarm system
of magpies

restless rest stop
black and white flutter
of hungry magpies

their end
in the name
magpies

mosquito
before going to bed
the mosquitoes too
have a snack

flute notes
on my bare arm
mosquito bites

life lessons
green pond of lotus lilies
home to our mosquitoes

male and female
in the contest of drummers
mosquitoes

mosquito nets
the only ones I know well
are in old poems

outdoors
called by a flute
mosquitoes

rain expected
at the screen mosquitoes
wanting in

taking our kids
for a swim
the mosquito and I

the night cut
into hot blocks
mosquitoes

the quiet
scratching the bite
of the mosquito

twanging
as if made of wires
mosquitoes

moth
bedside visitor
drawn to my lamp
a pale moth

dusty omens
from other worlds
moth messengers

osprey
lunchtime
the osprey dives
into the water

lunchtime
the osprey finds its reflection
contains a fish

pelicans

blessed
a low fly-over
of pelicans

end of summer
pelicans fly lower
over a wave

family dining
on a calm sea
pelicans

fourth of July
along the remote coast
a parade of pelicans

isle to island
the sea view stitched
by pelicans

lifting fog
a line of pelicans closer
to the waves

on their rock
by the rented house
pelicans land

smoothing the water
pelicans glide just behind
the breakers

three o'clock news
pelicans fly lower
over the waves

wedges of blue sky
diving into the sea
pelicans

young again
amid the most ancient
pelicans

rabbits
catching rabbits
under the setting moon
another poem

distant relatives
three rabbits gaze
at the full moon

looking for its mate
a lone rabbit watches
the lowering moon

mild and wild
in a grassy meadow
the rabbit's eyes

missing mass
seven rabbits
on my path

seabirds
shaping the rock
sharp shadows
of terns

wearing the wrong name
the grace of the shore bird
killdeer, killdeer

seals and sea lions
at high tide
one under water
seal rock

articulate snoring
sea lions sleep in
conversations

barking rocks
up close they become
a covey of seals

beach peace
yet over a flat rock
two seals fight

beach sand
gradually warming
the sleep of seals

breakfast on the wharf
harbor seals come to check out
our menu

cry of sea lions
lost in the mist
all those years

ebbing tide
on the flat rock
one more seal

end of summer
air hangs heavy over
a decaying seal

foggy morning
the sleeping of the seals
in closed eyes

high tide
the flat rock where seals sleep
white water waves

high tide over
the rock where seals slept
small waves

human voices
the rocks awake
as seals

incoming tide
the far rock becomes
a seal's body

incoming tide
the seal floats
off the rock

incoming tide
it floats a rock free
of a seal

low tide
the rock smooth and wet
with seals

low tide
yet all the sea
in the seal

making the trip
in an easy and relaxed manner
harbor seals

noisy new neighbors
down in the sea cove
migrating seals

on the beach
first letter of a poem
'c' a curled seal

one small rock
the baby seal recognized
by mom

rolling over
an incoming boat scares
the seals

rolling over
the white baby seal seems
to wave to me

seal dreams
their sleeping rock covered
by small waves

sea lion's mouth
the dawn inside the yawn
salmon pink

sea lions barking
in the sneeze's echo
another music

seal sleep
sliding on the slippery slope
sea stacks

swear words
slash the tranquil bay
fighting seals

the rock
that looks like a seal
covered with them

the tide turning
one sea lion slides
off a rock

unable to forget
the face in the driftwood
with seal brown eyes

visitors
counting the sea lions
in *their* cove

white brown and black
in tranquil bay the seals
are integrated

sea shells
a round mouth
on whorls of a conch's
deep calling

a round mouth
on whorls of a conch
the depths of the sea

doors to the sea
the pearly gates
of the moon shell

ear shell
the voice of the sea
whorled by a conch

in the conch
a whiff of the sea
deep voice

lips to a shell
the voice of the sea
in my breath

lips to a shell
the voice of the sea
whorls the conch

loaning breath
to the conch shell's whorls
voice of the sea

sea view
the snail's operculum
fingernail thin

tide pool colors
from under a rock
the periwinkle

sheep
coughing
the flock of sheep by starlight
a big gray blanket

sea fog
over the meadow sheep
an unpainted barn

twisted in wool
the life of a sheep
story of my fingers

snails
cut-down redwood
slowly over the year rings
a snail trail

homeless but happy
living on borrowed leaves
the slug

laying down a path
for the moon to follow
the garden snail

the snail
without a leg to stand on
passes me

whorls of a rose
loaned to the snail
eating it

snakes
a dead branch
then I remember this is
rattlesnake country

dried stream
its path made by a snake
twisting between rocks

eye to eye
the snake grows larger
wiser

just a shed skin
yet something of the snake
is still there

rattlesnake season
the only real danger is
in the newspaper

snake den rocks
even the dried grasses
have triangular heads

stream bed
once a snake of water
ran here

Werner shaving
a snake comes out to challenge
its rival – a razor

sparrows
day going
far behind the sparrow
its chirping

earthquake in LA
the sparrows unconcerned
over a sick bird

get-well visitor
a sparrow on the porch
poops and leaves

just ripe
the whole sparrow family
in my grapes

landing
the curve of a sparrow
to the earth

picnic
sparrows pick in horse dung
for the best parts

summer weekend
the swallow family also
has house guests

the earth
flying by
a sparrow

to catch a cat
sparrows steal drinks
from his dish

spiders
a night of rain
a spider repairs a web
with spangles

a spider's web
hanging in the wind chime
sunset colors

bugs and all
the garden belongs
to the spider

outdoor tea
the blue jay gets protein-rich
spiders

ship's rigging
holding fast
a spider web

spider legs
shaping the web
in an arch

tea ceremony
among the guests on a web
a spider

starfish
curve of the sea
fitting into the dome of sky
starfish

in the tide pool
the child's eager hand
a starfish

starfish
all the days of its life
going into a gull

swallows
a flutter of wings
bridging the river
swallows' nests

sea view properties
where no one lives
swallow nests

seen from below
the swallows' nests seem
fluffy birds

summer comes
filling the swallow's nest
with tiny noises

under the bridge
swallows' mud nests
ideas for new pots

water animals
mouths
dissolving rock faces
abalone

silent bells
in the sea
jellyfish

where the moon sets
a play of dolphins
in the silver path

whales
eclipse
touched by the eye
of a passing whale

hammock view
as it swings a whale
dives into the deep

more whales
company comes
for dinner

spangles
in the glare of the sun
a whale breeches

wild animals
badger lady
unknown center
of a dance

mountain stream
the raccoon washes his paws
in the moon

underground animals
bringing into earth
its very own grass
the gopher

light in the hairs
of the mole's nose
pushing dirt

oh the heat
gophers nibble the roots
of ice plants

SUMMER Plants

apples
a blush
on the child's cheek chewing
an apple

rites of childhood
eating green apples
getting so sick

up from the ground
and out on a limb
green apples

bamboo
a gesture
of a slanted bamboo
in my hand

a slap in the face
cutting back the bamboo
reddens the skin

bamboo breeze
the flutter of leaves
as it grows

bamboo leaves
on the porch boards
yamabuki shadow

pushing through earth
sheath on sheath the dew
of bamboo sprouts

berries
biting the strawberry
the taste of my tongue
in the sun

blackberry sun
dark places by the river
in jam jars

finding out
blue berries
secrets

blueberry pickers
in the bucket's melody
their songs

strawberry
another red tongue
on mine

strawberries
your tongue tasting
mine

the best of the jam
found later behind a tooth
raspberry seeds

bushes
chewed by deer
shoots of the thicket
do just that

desert sages
offering up to me
their differences

distant gray
rocks of the cliffs
now sagebrush

for children
hiding under the snow bush
summer coolness

giant berries in bloom
only your eyes can eat
rhododendrons

over-grown
the drooping azalea sits
with me on the bench

rhodie buds
the nipple pink
opens

triumphant return
on both sides of the road
oleanders

wild bush
seeing deep inside a flower
my sexual parts

cacti
all the hot colors
pink, magenta and red
in cactus flowers

in the rain
the cholla cactus gives
up its gray

daisies
a chill
the daisy trembles
in a sea breeze

a daisy chain
love too is hard to keep
together

a picket fence
blossoming daily
daisies

daisies
the wind bends one
into my hand

earth
giving itself
to a daisy

fireworks
at twilight a field
of daisies

moonset
the daisies nod
in a deep bow

nodding to daisies
I miss the bus but not
the wind

spotlighted
the wild daisies
high on a cliff

the sun's eye
in every meadow
daisies

toe nail polish
the daisy wears
yellow

ferns

ferns
making sweet music
shoulders

summer bracken
the shape of the spots
on the resting fawn

wild rivers
the joy unfurls
in ferns

flowers

a blur
among the flowers
bird song

a mind of its own
the Jerusalem Sage extends
forceful flowers

art show
true winners in the parking lot
small flowers

as children
they made dolls for us
hollyhocks

brightening flowers
the somber depth of evening
a cooler wind

cobblestones
paving the courtyard
geranium petals

crystal vase
even the flowers
have a moon

cut gladiolus
who remembers to open
each new floret

even when old
marigolds leave the skin smell
of my childhood

flowers
flowing with sex
the smell

flowers and flutes
in the flood of the sea
a beauty of wind

flowers opening
the air is curved
with birdsong

footsteps
on the beach path
tiny flowers

garden pillows
inviting one to rest here
beds of carnations

gardenias
no matter where they are
dancing – jazz music

growing up
to learn that a snowball
is a flower

her garden
so well-dressed
in foxgloves

hydrangeas
the flowers let in
sky color

if flowers spoke
zinnias would have
a broad accent

magnolia
its beauty falling
in non-silence

on a crape neck
the softness of flowers
in a lei

once mowed
the lawn burst into pink
phlox

our friendship
passed back and forth
in flowers

peonies
painted in the lushness
of heavy oils

poppies
a child leaves in the garden
red shoes

private garden
a fountain splashes
blue flowers

raised fists
the power salute
of dahlias

sheltered by trees
the power of the sea
in the flowers

shut in
your whole garden
in my vase

snapdragons
grown best by the neighbor
the bossy one

snapdragons
yes!
a mother-in-law

summer slow days
the four o'clocks open
earlier each time

summer vacation
the teacher doesn't know
the flower's name

sweet red
the cup of nectar
a small fountain

the first
boat builders
flowers

the gift of life
one day at a time
from the hibiscus

the pull of flowers
the photographer stops
at the loudest ones

they'll never grow there
the look on mom's face before
my morning glories

thickest
along the unused road
forget-me-nots

vegetable garden
bordered on one side
by honeysuckle

white shade
deep in the forest
Canada violets

fruits

apricots
fine hairs on the firm flesh
around his mouth

apricots
late in summer the sun
enters my mouth

childhood nightmare
bushels of cherries waiting
to be canned

designed to be
shaped to the human hand
a cluster of grapes

home alone
the banana ripens
on the table

olives
one on each finger
of the drunk

raisin country
in the rows of rain
empty vines

round faces
even matching dimples
in the cherries

who touched her?
falling under the tree
a green plum

work of days
sliding through the mouth
ripe fruits

grass

10 minute parking
the pampas grass waves
good-bye

bleached grass
all the yellow has gone
back to the sun

dune grass
perfect or not it holds
the sand hill

earth
flowing upward
ripened grass

earth
out of the earth
nameless grass

earth
turning around
dune grass

golden grass
bent to the earth by
passing summer

goose grass
a breeze goes
where it will

grass growing
the dried up waterfall is
still damp

grass fire
warmth in spring turns
to August heat

his dry humor
the grass shrivels
over his grave

music
in the grass
lovers

part plant
and part hummingbird
the fuchsia

purple grasses
the sun sets into
its familiar

saving sunlight
pampas grass plumes
back-lighted

sea meadows
waves on which I walk
rank grasses

soup smell
stirred by the sea wind
summer grass

speaking in whispers
the scythe swishes through
long grass

summer grass
sea wind petting
a great animal

summer grass
their heavy heads wave
as seas

the path
where prayers go
long grass

unbroken
the fence of grass
bent with dew

waiting for darkness
the roots of slender grass
no wind

grains
bowing to the wind
with the bounty of grain
the barley

corn fields
ripening the heat
golden yellow

days of summer
raked into piles
hay

earth
in the ears
of corn

growing slowly
over a field of barley
summer clouds

immigrants
settling around small houses
buckwheat

into the seaside cliff
patches of buckwheat
moonset

sun and sea
entering a wheat field
my teeth

sunshine
the ochre earth climbs
a wheat stalk

herbs

airy fairy flowers
the strong flavor of pickles
in the dill

arnica
the lacy food of bears
and pain

cliff side
the arnica grows higher
than my head

fake coolness
in a glass of ice water
peppermint

protected
in the summer night
spearmint

guided home
in the summer dark
arrowroot

moving off the road
before on-coming cars
horsemint

kelp

bullwhip kelp
among the floating bulbs
one electric

cilantro blooming
tonight's dinner must be
Mexican

curved green
the incoming wave brings
kelp to the beach

far island
kelp bed home
to strangers

islands with palms
on the North Coast
at low tide

kelp bed
the barrier reef's
calm seas

kelp beds
rising and wavering
as they grow

low tide
the purple sea grass dyes
the blue rocks

lupine and poppies
edging the steep rock
laver and sea palms

night ocean
in a kelp bed
calm

seaweed
adding a new note
to the flute

the forest
deep in the river
swaying grass

lawn
long day
so much to do yet
grass to cut

new mown hay?
my neighbor just mowed
his two acre lawn

Saturday morning
the scrape of a razor
smell of fresh-cut grass

summer solstice
laughter across the lawn
drifts down to the sea

the long day
grass growing
on the lawn

unable to sleep
a neighbor waters his lawn
at midnight

leaves
a fallen leaf
at least in its death
there is beauty

back and forth
leaf shadow weaves
over the loom

bending without wind
the green leaves accept
a sudden shower

leafy canopy
many fingers shadow
tree rings

summer leaves
giving one more sound
to the storm

summer leaves
in the full moon
a smoky tree

lilies

a lily
preaching by the road
brighter thoughts

dried up now
the stream of lilies bloom
in a brown meadow

lily pad
ripples in the pond
as flower petals

lovely yes
but isn't it lonely
being a lotus?

new owners
of the oldest barn
calla lilies

orange skies
at evening remembering
the daylily

stretching out
in a patch of sunlight
tiger lilies

the lily bends
a drop of dew
arrives home

the sun loans
its purest radiance
the lotus lily

unrolling
each day
the calla lily

melons

asking a friend
to carry the watermelon
take half

dinosaur eggs
the scavenger hunt prize
striped watermelon

eating watermelon
spitting seeds as far as
good manners go

muskmelon
dew gathers on the vine
another one

muskmelon
holding in its own juice
the summer sun

the flavor improves
on a wooden porch in the heat
watermelon

this hot day
how cool the earth
inside a melon

watermelon
need a fence and a hot day
to taste the best

moss

a new language
written in my oldest books
mildew

on a journey
resting under a large tree
green moss

other days
of high water marks
the bleached moss

with a brush
the old pine tree paints
itself with moss

oaks

growing
as great stones
ancient oaks

live oaks
so still afternoons
growing golden

native live oaks
the first inhabitants
welcome in the hills

oak afternoon
around the granite rocks
a solid stillness

sunshine rains
down the mountain ravine
golden oaks

twisted thread
inside the oak makes
itself strong

pines

among sugar pine
we are the mountains
in us

a tearing sound
a pine cone opens
to the heat

church spire
dwarfed by pine trees
the older snags

fame
the pines of China come
into my garden

friendly
the pine shares its fragrance
mid-day shade

pines
at the edge of the sky
music to the eye

pine canopy
in the hammock
a clean smell

pine and cypress
swinging between them
a hammock

pine and cypress
swinging with the breezes
a hammock

pine fire
smoke leaving
tree-shaped

moonlight
curved by a pine needle
piercing beauty

reaching for sun
the great pine's shadow
shapes the tree

rubbish fires
salvaging the smells
of pine

shore pine
by my one day
older

striking pillars
sunshine on incense cedars
worthy companions

tall ridge of pines
divine hieroglyphics
written with the sun

the tea
in a pine needle cup
coolness

the wait
looking up from a book
a pine branch nods

poppies
field of poppies
how far we walked to get
sun burnt noses

red hot pokers
into the heat
red hot pokers glow iridescent
with hummingbirds

setting fire red
against the green of leaves
red-hot pokers

redwoods
a grove of redwoods
the congregation's prayers
taller now

art show
true winners in the parking lot
the redwoods

call of the flute
answer of drums
among redwoods

dancing
from cloud to trees
island drums

earth
flowing into its other self
the tallest redwood

gallery sitting
redwoods in the window
the biggest visitors

leaning on a stick
the wobbly view up to
the redwood's top

memorial service
swaying redwoods
groan

new growth
on the redwoods
Kronos concert

on the stage
redwood needles
flute music

in the company
of trees with itself
redwood elbows

ochre earth
holding itself in
the redwood

redwoods
their line drawn
in brown ink

redwoods
the prayers go straight
to heaven

redwood ritual
driving through a tree
2400 year-old kids

shakuhachi tones
younger redwoods sway
first

Soda Springs
a Disney World
of old redwoods

the giant redwood
a pain in the neck from
looking upward

the redwood snag
climbing into the sky
with bare limbs

unable to draw
we stand open mouthed
under redwoods

where the giant fell
violets
and redwood sprouts

roses

as if nodding
yes! the old fashion rose
drops a petal

from a bush
the scent of roses
morning mist

garden border
around the courthouse
peace roses

good neighbors
on the unused fence
a climber rose

holding up
the deserted oil well
climber rose

morning dew
even my toes are changed
to rose petals

rosebud
the name of the deer
that eats them all

vase water
a happening of roses
lilies and daffodils

the day's length
entering the rose
as it opens

unable to open
as full as a rose
the bell

warm valley night
the scent of roses
my only blanket

sea oats

nestlings learn to fly
at the same time sea oats
start to ripen

sea oats and lupine
the backyard carpeting
needs mowing

summer breezes
sea oats being stroked
by a great hand

thinning fog
the edge of the cliff fringed
with sea oats

succulents

a breeze
shaping the yucca blossom
bird shadow

a great pot
of green leaves with thorns
the unknown succulent

ice plants
blown from the sea
in a cold wind

yucca's cool green
attracts the white birds
flowers

sunflowers

dusk
sunflowers in a vase
rearrange themselves

garden secrets
the sunflower turns
where two whisper

middle of the land
the Kansas sunflower looks
both east and west

seventh drawing
I begin to feel the sunflowers
belong to me

waiting for dawn
I sit beside the tallest
sunflower

thistles
along the coast
clusters of communities
lupine and thistle

prickly – yet
how gently dew is held
by the summer thistle

staring at the thistle
her divorce story reminds
me of mine

tall and elegant
in the chewed-down pastures
thistles

trees
a dusty hike
entering the cool waters
of deep tree shade

a sea breeze
among the mountain trees
it follows us here

alone with trees
far away and unseen
a chain saw

an artist
painting her own house
adding maples

balmy breezes
fan out in green fringe
palm trees

coolness
held aloft on limbs
summer trees

coolness
shaded from the sun
summer grove

deep in the woods
green shadows shade
to blue

drizzled over rocks
something about the trees
edging the sea

drum and flute
the silence of trees
breathing together

knot holes
wood turning around
in itself

prayers
going up the trees
guitar chords

shade warmth
from the top of the tree
blown down

sighs
redwoods applaud
shakuhachi player

silence
where the trees still
are wise

still flute
music familiar
to the trees

storm winds
lowered down to earth
falling twigs

the drape
of water over rock
a broken tree

the hillside leans
with a row of trees
the wind

tied to a tree
humming in the wind
a hammock

tourists
staring at tall trees
being watched

tree shade
the mercy of god
takes shape

trees still
listening to the flute
low notes

trees sway
the performers blessed
by evening breezes

under the tree
in the full moon
morning tea

valley oaks
in the curve of a limb
hillsides

wind blows
from mossy trees
stories

vegetables

as if a jewel
from the good earth
polished eggplant

before pop-tab cans
green pea pods opening
the same sound

corn on the cob
everyone at the table
becomes a child

days
made of zucchini
long and hot

eating green peas
raw with the taste of the pod
under the thumbnail

in my mouth
the warm sun
of a tomato

new potatoes
boiled but tasting
yet of earth

promontory
pushing up into the sun
yellow salsify

the water sprays
into their coolness
cucumbers

weeds
beach path
where we no longer go
bindweed

bindweed
morning brings me back
to this beach

blown by wind
yet the dandelions
face the sun

camp fire
reflected in cliff walls
monkey faces

campus green
summer weeds grow
on the paths

first steps
walking to the beach
loosestrife

heavy fog
after weeks of blooming
the foxgloves bend

marijuana buds
the osprey cries hovering over
the sun-warmed road

old woman
alone on the steep path
loco weeds

shade light
blooming under the pines
wintergreen

strong willed
the dandelion in asphalt
the woman who pulls it

steep beach path
carefully watched over
by monkey face flowers

summer garden
weeding done by sparrows
in wild disarray

swept away
shoulder-high yellow
of Scotch broom

switchback
coming around the mountain
monkey face flowers

end of summer
tall and bright in the fields
of thistle

on the path
to a picture perfect day
Indian paintbrushes

time on my hands
the flowers I found among
the weeds

wanting to shout
the summer weeds overcome
the flowerless bed

why was it made?
the poison oak*
just being itself
                    *Rhus diversiloba

willows

curving
stones from the cliff
the willow craft

in prior lives
willows were kids who loved
green tents

on the beach
a willow boat
blooms

wood

a porch warms
the wood sings a song
of tall trees

a hole in the log
asks to be my pillow
hold my dreams

ripples in the wind
bleached dune grass
silvered driftwood

wood to wood
the flute brings the trees
into swaying

wood on wood
flute drums and trees
my echoing heart

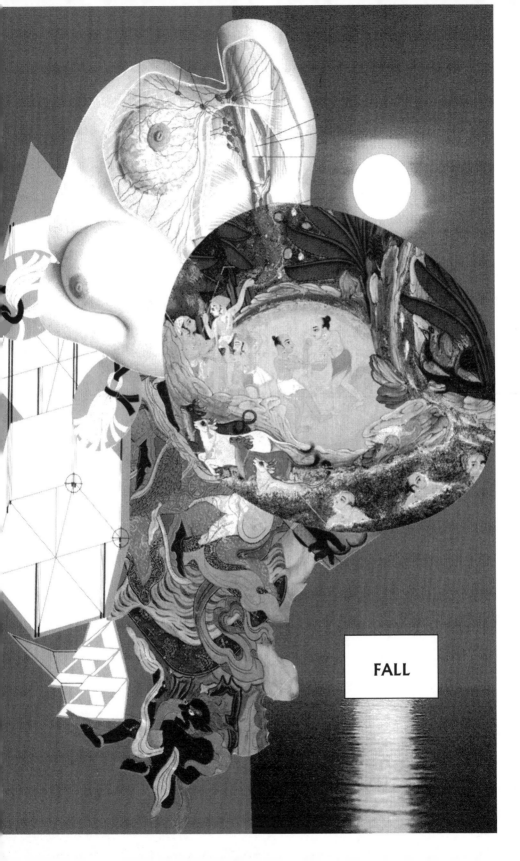

FALL

FALL Moods

abandoned

train gone
feeling abandoned while
waiting for mine

acceptance

a dark moon
I could live with that
I think

a fallen leaf
even in its death
it is lovely

autumn begins
with the fading light
old age is easier

caught
in her eyes
his words

how patiently
the moon accepts
its eclipse

lunar eclipse
seeing again wrinkled skin
on my hands

passing in the night
the moon and my shadow
all the planets

warming
her sweet face
gray

unsaid
on her lips
yes

alone

alone now
the bed is rumpled
and awake

alone on the rock
there seems to be something
the sea wants

autumn evening
the oldest book is open
on my lap

deep thoughts
a lone man stares
out to sea

house spider
tonight I feel
more alone

in the dark
music for each alone
togetherness

moon time
alone in the house
with surf roar

music
how it gathers
the lonely

one autumn evening
trying on his wife's hosiery
home alone

purple
the crazy plant stands
for loneliness

the heavy sweater
alone
it is enough

being needed
waking up
the setting moon seems to
want
us to watch

up
because it called to me
the moon sets

blessed
1.8 million
the art center richer
by its redwoods

after sunset
the glow in the west
on your cheek

burnt clay
faces of my ancestors
sparkling with fire

by the sea
mountains brought down
by my eyes

super moon
fall's abundance
golden round

the element
on which the living float
blessed ancestors

the perfect full moon
sometimes in old age
I get things right

coping
buying something
the image of youth
in a pocketbook

cloudy skies
for the eclipse more
chocolate cake

even dead
the cockscomb flowers upright
in perfect order

it comes
from her knees
the giggle

once more
the forced laugh
thin wrists

survivor
I alone hear
the owl

after his stroke
each of his haiku
better than ever
for George Knox

in daylight
the gift of his leaving
this tenderness

depression

fallen leaves
each year repeating
these same feelings

low clouds
when you think of it
all is a wall

scattering leaves
the wind cannot blow away
the blues

Spanish moss
the shape of melancholy
in the trees

surf roar
unable to quell
the weeping

weeping
the river recognizes itself
on my face

desire

autumn seas
the desire to travel
home

getting hungry
moonset thoughts
of cheese

disappointment

morning fog
my dead parent's disapproval
gathers in valleys

scattering leaves
the autumn cannot blow away
disappointment

dreaming

filling a wish
money exchanged
for a dream

dreaming
the things seen
by the moon

dreamy
still her body makes
promises

the dream
of killing the neighbor's dog
my cat dead

failure

for grandma
the fan that holds autumn
folded wrong

failed marriage
the end of the years
in Lemon Cove

fear
drums
shadows begin to dance
at sunset

no one home
in my body on the table
my fears

scary
her scarecrow resembles
the man next door

the fears
fog hangs in a valley
just ahead

forgetting
autumn evening
forgetting that I too
will die

getting older
autumn
I've fallen in love
for the last time

cinnamon and sugar
the red-headed girl never
thought she'd get old

old age
the moon rises
in the morning

old clothes
what does she see
herself wearing

older now
the moon is pulled down
into the sea

a yellow toenail
in old age the moon sinks
into cold seas

hope
already
a gibbous moon
I feel richer

during the eclipse
no visitors expected and yet
turning on the porch light

future seasons
the glass waiting to be filled
with wine days

illness
autumn days
the flute with my breath
grows feeble

because of pain
the morning moon set
itself down gently

I swine
thou flu
two autumns

sick again
the moon sets in the sea
blood red

sleepy again
full-moon madness
passes

lonely
autumn evening
in a letter to dad
the long postscript

how quiet the eaves
since the fledglings left
kids' bedroom

haven't written
waves half-a-world away
rush to the shore

longing
a hole
in the ordinary world
a missing pet

a thin thread
wanting to give all
and let go

moon shine
I see my old home
where no one lives

on the wane
the no-moon evening
and she's gone

tourist
coming to his home village
autumn

missing
gallery-sitting
the pain of losing him
waits at home

missing cat
missing everything
I've ever missed

missing him
all the brave thoughts
about living alone

still missing
a feather found
for a lost cat

the beautiful day
with the empty hole
of missing him

memories
by her portrait
the two lilies remind me
of her hands

mindless
mindless
driving mindlessly
the mindless valley

mourning
a death
the eclipsed moon sets
dark

autumn chill
writing the name of one dead
stiff and crooked

autumn leaves
the unspoken number
of missing things

bowed by grief
while I feel the loss
redwoods straighter

pillar of sorrow
the hours alone
touching it

temperature
59 degrees and she was
ninety-five

there's a name
for what bends my shoulders
bone deep grief

thinking of her
in the silence of loss
wind chimes

mysteries
autumn
the sound beyond
spelling

a laugh
what was said
just before?

buttons
what have they to do
with butts

fading light
yet on her face
a warmth

fences sliding
down the hillside
where does time go?

in silence
all those no longer here
gather around

look again!
how many moonrises
is a life allowed

moon eclipse
how does it look
to the dying?

only her mirror
sees her thus
thin and young

silence
after something falls
a coming apart

where does she go
the girl in gum boots
in the fog

wind in the bamboo
where do they come from
these notes

reality check
after the eclipse
counting the hairs
which have fallen

174

feeling important
and then the moon sets
into dark seas

scattered ashes
no place for a cross
in autumn wind

regrets
his ideas so right
for all the wrong reasons
follow me

how she loved dolls
the now grown daughter
childless

no sons
his baseball mitt catches
only dust

remembering
autumn
our forgetting even
to remember

forgetting
last night's dreams
fallen leaves

her qualities
so rare in the family
cheerful goodness

it is hard
when you think about it
remembering the dead

moonset
in a still dark meadow
the memories

moon radiance
it is hard to remember
it is sun shine

remembering
all the family at my wedding
now dead

strangers
on the city sidewalks
one has his laugh

shame
earth's dark
shadow covers the moon
someone banned

in shame
stars before the full moon
fade and go

my name
in my father's address book
misspelled

spitting from the bridge
grandma stops showing off
when mom comes along

suicide
dangerous weather
such a perfect day for stepping
off a cliff

tired
getting tired
of gallery-sitting
the mouse runs out

understanding
her ankles
so far from her face
the beauty

her tomorrow
is only now
yesterday

new season new looks
funny old haiku
poetry

stages
we pass between
actors

the star
on her the sweater
fits

the ugly coat
reflected on her face
it's there!

unsure
a scoop neck
suddenly he is
unsure

thoughts
about a cotton jersey
wrinkled

unsure
passing over a face
a cloud

waiting
a day waiting
for visitors to show up
a lost cat

the moon
so long in the dark
the cat meows

waiting
for the question
stilled breath

wisdom
all his words
and she knows how
silly they are

blowing not blowing
the wisdom of a dried leaf
rests on the ground

destiny questions
answers in the golden moon's
watery path

eyes shut
that's the way to buy
a sweater

her
comfort zone
looking back

the hat
is at its best
off

what word
makes a woman
shy

worry
in two years
when the moon is eclipsed
where will I be

moon eclipse
the cat's worried meow
tangles my feet

the stare
a line drawn
to the future

worried
even the sweater
wrinkles

FALL Occasions

All Souls' Day
all souls day
light still flickers in the
painting
made by a friend

all souls day
the pumpkin candle
burns on the altar

all saints' day
the balloon and muslin ghost
is gone

All Souls' Day
no one in the cemetery
   - not one -

arrival of autumn
a holiday decoration
corn shocks and pumpkins
by Hallmark

arrival
of the first cricket
august autumn

autumn
drawing me closer
to the scare crow

equinox
the ocean fills both sides
of the bay

first view of autumn
from the mountain peaks
bare rocks

it looks new
in the moonlight
autumn

elections
election day
only the last daisy can tell
Bush, Gore, Bush, Gore. . .

election day
the whales chose
to go south

end of autumn
autumn ends
leaf on withered leaf
in blowing snow

departing autumn
footsteps buried
in frosted leaves

end of autumn
nine snowy egrets
whiten the rocks

end of autumn
the dead tree closer
to winter

late in autumn
who is this asking
about death?

harvest moon
harvest
the golden grain color
in the moon

the harvest moon
bringing in the pumpkins
yet on the porch

Halloween
after Halloween
the rich shopping for bargains
turn into witches

autumn wind
whiter and colder
in the ghost

black and orange
the crow's eye
on the persimmon

evening wind
the lost kite blows out
of ghost canyon

Halloween
even the stormy seas
are scary

night of the dead
in the dead of the night
all of the dead

on the cliff
pumpkin faces
moonlight

pumpkins
rising out of the field
harvest

summer thin
the scarecrow on Halloween
a ghost

sunset glow
shaped to the eyes and mouth
of a pumpkin

waiting to enter
the county courthouse
jack-o-lanterns

Thanksgiving Day
after Thanksgiving
the refrigerator light
goes dark

Thanksgiving Day
seeing an old neighbor
after her surgery

Thanksgiving
the pocket beach fills
at high tide

Thanksgiving feast
around the wooden table
friends — bread

Thanksgiving
rainstorm and power outage
our blessings

Thanksgiving
rocks covered with seaweed
swell with the tide

Thanksgiving day
the great blue heron
nabs a gopher

Veteran's Day

homeless vets
sleeping in the shadows
a war memorial

on the vet's face
through tears in the flag
slashes of sun

remembering the dead
one gull comes gliding
out of the sea fog

remembering the dead
something moves the silk
of the flag

the Vietnam Vet
in his eyes
my debt

FALL Celestial

breeze

low notes
the woods' breezes
smell strange

tapping my shoulder
the low branch brings
a cool breeze

bright weather

blue sky day
drawing autumn leaves
in a circle

bright weather
shaking the house
bending trees

clouds

a scribbled sky
in the wispy clouds
a clear blue mind

autumn sky
the gravel path puddles
with clouds

over the sea
far from mountains
cloud-country moon

the moon
obscured by clouds
brightens the sky

thinning clouds
the moon slips free
into the sea

comets

shooting star
in my haste to see it
shooting pain

darkness

darker now
yet the flute master's
sound glows

darkness
coming from the flute
the low notes

the shadow bends
blowing sand lengthens
the coming darkness

out of darkness
the thrill of flutes
drumming

dawn

dawn
the full moon goes dark
transparent

morning light
the dark moon
fades

past full
the moon sets
into dawn pink

sunrise
in the eclipsed moon
darkness fades

sunrise
the silver moon turns
to gold

up at dawn
how to make an autumn day
last longer

warming colors
the moon nears the sea
dawn

dew
the misty moon
leaves the earth
dew-wet

dew richly laid
every drop has
a moon

dusk
autumn dusk
meeting on the road
a long shadow

dusk spare
the autumn evening comes
home to roost

new moon
as if new
the perfect moon
comes to earth

evening
coming together
evening clouds
flute players

fog
corners of the moon
a deep orange set into blue
morning fog

spirit husk
the sea moon fades
into the fog

frost
dew comes down
from the river of heaven
first frost

full moon
a bit of sky
drops the full moon
into the sea

a golden haze
closer to the sea
the full moon

a full moon
no other ship sails
upon the sea

a sliver of light
the full moon sinks
into earth shadow

behind pine trees
the golden moon has the eyes
of a jack-o-lantern

bright enough
to write a poem
the full moon

closer now
to the full moon
an empty heart

full moon
the darkness on the other side
of night

Orion
and the full moon
sea journey

sleepless
with the full moon
keeping me company

sleepy again
the full moon madness
passes

swinging north
the full moon dissolves
into winter

the full moon
brightens the stillness
of the sea

the full moon
going to bed with
half of it

the gift exchange
radiance of the full moon
and a still sea

the radiance
of the dark cat
full moon

light
blue lights
the slow rhythms
of low notes

first light
the edge of the moon
whitens

morning
the returning light fades
on the moon

lunar eclipse
a squeak of light
on the dark moon
eclipse

dropping
toward the sea
eclipsed moon

eclipsed moon
only a sliver of light
cradles it

eclipsed moon
the light goes out
into stars

fragile light
the eclipsed moon
stays dark

less light
the roundness of the moon
reddens

light
in distant places
eclipsed moon

lunar eclipse
out of dark skies
rain falling

morning light
the moon sinks
still dark

morning lightens
yet the eclipsed moon
stays dark

night takes the moon
then gives it back to me
lunar eclipse

over great distances
the shadow of something
makes
a red moon

sea colors
the eclipsed moon
breaks free

the darkness fades
the eclipsed moon over-taken
by morning

moon
17th day moon
the missing side
filled with wind

a cup of tea
and the huge moon
comes closer

almost holy
other lives on the moon
craters

a quiet sea
as if made for the moon
to find itself

around the earth
writing on the moon
the bonding

as the moon fades
light returns to the little
that's left

a tree
or leaping rabbit
moon pictures

a wisp of light
all that remains
of the moon

bone white – bone dry
the moon rises and sets
in the sea

bright red
the blue planet's shadow
on the moon

clear
cellophane
moonlight

closer now
the moon arrives
on its silver path

dark edge
the moon rises
into the sun

far out at sea
pulled by the moon
fishing boats

from old to new
a valley's journey to the sea
the moon

is it round?
the light goes out
in part of the moon

lop-sided moon
the white of many boats
rush to its loss

marking earth
the silver sea path
the moon follows

moon path
from south to north
it sweeps the sea

moving closer
to the stove
the moon warms

nearly home
the moon slides into
the Pacific Ocean

older now
light drains away
from the moon

replacing the candle
a special moon comes
in the window

rough-scarred
but far away
the perfect moon

tea colored
the moon comes closer
to my cup

the autumn wind
takes leaves from the tree
brings it the moon

the eyeball moon
gazes into the sea
its own glow

the lightness
drawn to the moon
soap bubbles

the distance
showing the moon
as perfect

white edged clouds
the new moon's dark belly
in a crescent of light

with the moon
night too disappears
into the ocean

writing it down
before it is lost
17th day moon

moon dust
a dust of light
cradles the moon
morning

it is not icy
so it must be silver
moon dust

moonlight
bound by night
writing pens move
in the moonlight

deep in the sea
the moon pulls the tides
fishing lines

it looks new
in the moonlight
calendar

mid-day
moonlight still lingers
in bright shadows

moonlight
follows a pine needle
piercing beauty

moonlight
wrapped in a blanket
one spot is still cold

the sound
of moonlight coming ashore
waves

moon rise
a friend who comes
on the sea's silver path
the full moon

closer now
the moon arrives
on its silver path

one color
on both sides of the earth
sunset – moonrise

moon set
a cold sea
the shrinking moon pales
before it sets

a long shadow
again the moon moves
into the light

a roar of waves
as the moon sinks
into the sea

a silver path
crosses the winter sea
the moon goes down

as with a will
the huge moon lowers
into the sea

before moonset
every thing bright
with meaning

candle glow
the setting moon
is warming

candle glow
the moon sinking into the sea
warms golden

clear skies
unable to hold back
the sinking moon

earth's curvature
the moon sets into
another darkness

eclipsed
the moon sets
as one new

into the sea
following its golden path
moonset

moonset
only a dusting of light
on one side

moonset
releasing into the sky
the stars

other worldly
the deep orange moon
is gone

sinking
the darkened moon
seems forever

so far away
our atmosphere flattens
the setting moon

sunrise
a warm glow covers
the setting moon

the moon sinks
into the roar of seas
a silver path

the setting moon
comes to a world
newly created

the setting moon
covered with clouds
sleepy

the setting moon
waves move aside
so it can enter

new moon
the sliver of light
clings to the bottom
so is it round

night
out of stillness
the night begins to play
wind chimes

quarter moon
quarter moon
yet the sea light
a wide path

rain
between showers
every puddle has
a moon

black and white
the storm rains down
hours of the night

rainstorm
the Big Dipper tilted
in our direction

wall to wall water
the autumn rains come
to the river

shorter days
autumn days
a trickle of slanted light
feeds me

the day shortens
as the beach deepens
its shadows

sky
17th day moon
the pearl of great price
in the morning sky

clear skies
unable to hold back
the sinking moon

deep skies
have taken the birds
rest of the sun

sky white
with heat only waves
come ashore

solar eclipse
after the eclipse
drops of dew are
full again

far away
solar eclipse in my home town
completely dark

light dimming
birds eat and run
before the eclipse

solar eclipse
sea fog rolls into
the half-light

solar eclipse
the old wound
hurts again

stars
autumn
seven sisters stars
not so lonely

back home
all the music returns
to the stars

dew comes down
from the river of heaven
earth stars

light from the moon
as it passes the stars
brightens

miracle of stars
on a full moon night
eclipse

morning light
the stars fade before
the darkened moon

watching
a full moon
a star falls

storm
wind-blown
she gives in after
the storm

sunset
at a slant
light into the autumn sea
of a day going

low purple sea
the sun sets into
its watery self

shadows
to grow old and lean
in the setting sun

sunset
deeper the flute
warms us

sunset
ink in the red pen
turns black

sunset
music colors
in the clouds

sun
autumn afternoon
the golden yellow sunshine
seems older

bright sun
on the long waves of autumn
end of a day

sea and sun
in their great depths
a subtle change

thunder and lightning
another news flash
of who won the election
thunder and lightning

tides
neap moon tides
the beach disappears
under the sea

phases of the moon
the tide rearranges the shore
to make it right

rising tide
suddenly the sky loses
the moon

sea thunder
round the cliffs
autumn tides

testing the tide
the evening light
rushes ashore

tides pulling
the moon into the sea
fishing boats

turning tide
a roar of water pulls
down the moon

twilight
darkness slipping in
water that cannot be still
twilight

waning moon
crests of waves
leaping into the sky
a waning moon

tug on a line
a waning moon pulls
the fishing boats

waning moon
a fullness resolved
by the skull

waning moon
lopsided but perfect
white skull

whirlwinds
sweeping up leaves
the whirlwind does it faster
the second time

twister!
afraid to watch the sky
afraid to move

wind
a thief
pushing open the window?
wind oh!

Basho's birthplace
the memory of him
in the clear wind

button missing
the cloudy day enters
my coat as wind

conversation
of flutes at sunset
the wind

even the wind
tries to expose
her breasts

wind storm
neighbor's wind chimes still
in my yard

FALL Terrestrial

beach

autumn
leaves on the beach
empty crab shells

autumn waves
high on the beach
something sleeps

early November
beside me in the sand
chilly shadows

full moon
shining on the beach sand
marked with bare feet

moonlit beach
we let our footprints
wash out to sea

on the beach
the moon sets
in the surf's roar

cliffs

from the cliff top
the moon sinks
into the mist

desert

desert dry
a river of rocks
flowing again

still hot
here in the desert
a lava foot

earth

arched brows
owning the earth
of eye acres

ashes to ashes
the moon turns
a dusty red

blurring the stars
handfuls of damp earth
farewell

bone white
the baby bowl filled
with earth

low notes
the earth still in
the shakuhachi

marking earth
the silver sea path
the moon follows

moonset
the earth forms itself
into meadow green

on earth
the warmth of a full moon's
golden glow

sea thunder
at the edge of the earth
autumn tides

unstable earth
its long shadow moves
over the moon

fields
the moon sets
in a frosty field
eclipse dark

hills
oak trees
the hills themselves
higher

landslide
landslide
the ash plume of
granite dust

mountain
autumn sharp
the rocky summits
of home

long shadows
walking toward the mountain
its longing for me

mountain peak
already in August
autumn in sight

mountain slopes
my rain
into your snow

seeing Fuji
on a rainy day
missing smiles

river
a dried up stream
an autumn wind blows
in its bed

autumn storm
the river running fast
and tree deep

coming forward
as a yellow tree
autumn river

low river
in Anderson Valley grapes
are very full

rivers
take us to our tears
their stony beds

the blue tongue
of God
autumn of river

weeping
the river recognizes itself
on my face

rocks
a secret
held by a rock
the black hole

coming home
the moon's radiance
on favorite stones

dark ancestor
of sea-claimed rock
exposed quartz vein

homage
to a ghost potter
Navajo rocks

moon tides
the big rock breathes
ocean spray

old friends
how different in rain
are the rocks

red leaves
warming the shadows
stream-deep rocks

rising tide
water on the rocks
covers the moon

rock shadow cool
coming over the dunes
in waves

shore rocks
washed by the sea
evening dark

stained dark
again the sea washes
island rocks

wave shaped
the rock teaches water
again this September

seas
a bit of sky
drops the full moon
into the sea

a quiet sea
as if made for the moon
to find itself

a roar of waves
as the moon sinks
into the sea

as one bathing
in the dark sea
a red moon

bubbles
above the sea foam
the golden moon

flames on the sea
the burning waters
of the setting moon

lightly pressing
sea surfaces flat
thin mists

kelp bed
the barrier reef's
calm seas

moonset
from the dark sea
another wave

moon chips
on the windy sea
white caps

moon set
a radiance of the line
between sea and sky

moon set
the roar of the sea
even louder

when a moon sets
where the sea was
a white stone

morning to night
in the embrace of tides
calm seas

sea light
shining on the bottom
of the moon

the oldest pilgrim
with stick and shell
the sea

the path shortens
approaching the sea
the golden moon

the restless sea
even adding the moon
gives no peace

the restless sea
even without a lullaby
sleep

the seaside
the other air
of a new face

weeping
the ocean flows again
on my face

waves
moon chips
on the windy sea
white caps

offering themselves
to the lopsided moon
crests of waves

sun dark
with the moon rising
a white wave

the full moon
brightens the stillness
in waves

the setting moon
waves move aside
so it can enter

waterfall
from the river
creating a curve
rock stains

waterfall
not the jacket but
her hair

wind
in the waterfall
white ghosts

FALL Livelihood

ancestors
autumn dusk
something comes down from
ancestor portraits

boats and fishing
17th day moon
dropping into the sea
19 boats

cirrus clouds
a net is cast
into the sea

crossing the creek
without my boat
pine shadow wind

eclipsed moon
brighter on the stormy seas
fisher lights

fallen
from the morning moon
19 fishing boats

lopsided day moon
fisher folk pulling in
heavy lines

moonset
the sparkles on the sea
fishing boats

cabin
closing the cabin
a pile of leaves grow
on the porch

closed-up house
on a bare branch hangs
a cocoon

replacing laughter
on the cabin porch
a flutter of leaves

candles
a lit candle
where the moon shines
there's fire

lighting a candle
the moon slips away
in a smoky cloud

lightning
the power of the storm
one candle

moonset
into the dawn burns
a candle

replacing the candle
the full moon comes
in the window

cemeteries
atop the coffin
a flutter of petals
an open Bible

bells tolling
his heartbeat moves
into the sky

cemetery
here the leaves lie
deeper

closer to mother
than we've been in years
after cremation

cremation smoke
above the earth
with spirits

dry humor
not even grass grows
over his grave

dictator
not even a tree grows
on his grave

earth
in a cedar box
into the tomb

graveyard wind
with the crosses of wings
returning the energy

grieving for him
lines raked in the sand
not quite straight

hour of cremation
eyes closed in prayer
in flames

leaves falling
I find no one else
in the cemetery

men kneeling
in the ancient burial pose
a long coffin

mother's cremation
the burning sensation
in my belly

on the grave
with no flower wreath
colorful leaves

river of mourners
flowing by the coffin
tears

rustic cemetery
only bracken bends
and browns

sunlight reflects
on the cedar coffin
a chill

tending the graves
the dirt under my nails
is just a beginning

their eyes closed
to a million dollar view
a seaside cemetery

the white cloth
over the death mask
forgiving

upright stones
under our sad faces
the bone grin

washing
the gravestone
warms

who lays the leaves
against the granite stone
the beetle's home

children
divorce
not wanting anything
except the kids

first frost
in my daughter's hair
my gray

still cold
spoons in the sandbox
empty

cooking
candling eggs
and now the moon is
transparent

egg candling
the eclipsed moon
is fertile

moonset
the shadow of a bowl
reaches out to me

sharing a hug
the tea kettle boils
and boils and boils

cleaning
brushing the mat
the shadow of a broom
a windblown tree

cleaning house
rearranging furniture
but he is still gone

feather duster
dark in his chair
his absence

he's back!
no, the feather duster
is in his chair

decorating
autumn leaves in her arms
one more on her shoe

found in the trash
the perfect basket
autumn flowers

gathering clouds
whine of the vacuum cleaner
sucks up dust

my best work done
I change my clothes
to empty the trash

overcast skies
when the chain saw revs up
it begins to rain

silver hair
now that she is gone
it is a treasure

clothes
a fashion statement
hung in the closet
hangs

ah!
even the fat lady looks
thin in this

baby alpaca
but the sweater belongs
to grandma

contest
who can make the t-shirt
smile?

clumps
of brown grass
her sweater

dancing lessons
leotards on the clothesline
in a high wind

full moon
pressed to my eye
contact lens

girls
changing
clothes

clothes
changing
girls

monocle
the full moon looks
back at me

moonlight
putting jewels on all
my fingers

moon more golden
adding jackets as it
sets

oops
another sweater
for a cold day

September moon
heavier now with
thicker pants

she is beautiful
the lady who stacks
folded shirts

shirts
to cover old fat
thin shimmer

shorter days
the clothesline doesn't reach
the sun

sweaters
still friendly
unsold

thin fabric
her boobs hidden
by a shoulder

wearing sunglasses
in the shade
her glow

wrinkles
in her t-shirt
giggles

younger now
grandma's sweater
$119.

death
a tearing wind
the pain being alone
without her

death notice
the storm clouds seem
more purple

death notice letter
the widower's comments
make me furious

her death
the stone she gave me
lies in my palm

she dies
of a massive heart attack
the evangelist

sunset
into a fog of tears
she is gone

entertainment
all over the planet
they join to watch the moon
eyes

autumn evening
coming from the buoy
deep bell tones

breathing
the moon in the glasses
goes up and down

cloudy skies
hearing of the eclipse
on the radio

coins
falling into the pond
the moon

football game
on the radio touchdown
no one hears me cheer

gorgeous moonset
in the warmest room is
the best view

half-time show
the tuba turns the leaves
red and gold

into clouds of cold
getting another blanket
for moon viewing

outdoor concert
the flute master warms
my ears

midnight
ah ankles and shoes
on the street

moon eclipse
people gather on the coast
to watch

moon eclipse
whale watching glasses
need adjustment

museum tired
before and behind me
countless ages

the same old moon
yet we sit in the cold to see
the eclipse

war museum
sitting down to still
my quaking knees

flutes
autumn days
the flute with my breath
migrating birds

bamboo
fingering the holes
from hot stones

end of the song
all the wooden holes closed
by fingers

given breath
the poetry
in the flute

notes from bamboo
in and out of the flute
his breath

the highest note
on the bamboo flute
a splinter

wind in bamboo
the heartbeat
of a shakuhachi

world journey
the bamboo flute
by way of Japan

foods and meals
a cup of tea
the setting moon warms
the coming winter

after the eclipse
cookies dipped in
hot cocoa

a wide grin
pumpkin seeds
in my mouth

continuing rain
a flock of grey-coated
mushroom hunters

dieting
the cup of cold coffee
autumn

eating leftovers
in my relationship corner
bandit-faced raccoons

eating licorice
folks at the concert of
flute music

full sun
we say grace before
breakfast

home alone
the banana ripens
on the table

housewarming
taking off her blouse
because of the wine

setting moon
as it enters the ocean
the aroma of tea

solar eclipse
cold sun's half darkness
I need more coffee

solar eclipse
my lips curve around
the Oreo

steaming tea
the full moon set
into thin clouds

tea colored
the moon comes closer
to my cup

wineglass
half-full and overflowing
with all that jazz

wine tasting
for the senior citizens' tour
a little more water

voodoo magic
the herbs hung in bundles
upside-down

friends
a friend who comes
on the sea's silver path
tonight's moon

haiku meeting
I sit outdoors
writing alone

my friend dies
preaching a gospel
I do not believe

rising to enter
deep in our conversation
the moon

funeral
after the funeral
thankful to be going
back to bed

autumn farewell
flowers without fragrance
as keepsake

candle shadows
in the silence of a flicker
a life

cold rain
huddled in the hearse
remorse

father's red carnations
beside mom's pink roses
as in life

furniture
a chair
bending in half
the stiff lady

after the moon eclipse
all the kitchen chairs
in wrong places

a mirror
on the west wall
goes dark

banging on mirrors
the eclipsed moon hears
and comes back

circling the light
a dark stone lantern
the darker bamboo

clean sheets
moon shine covers my bed
with new dreams

doctor's office
among the antique furniture
a skeleton

from chair to chair
following the moonset
into the sea

frost
the moon shines on my bed
last camp-out

hiss of sand
in the hourglass
nightfall

sinking to earth
the full moon arrives
on my bed

the easy life
the airport attendant brings
a wheelchair

ghosts
player piano
at the Ghost Ranch
a visitor

watching the ghost
all the shapes of a woman
in the wind

heating devices
an act of faith
in total darkness
striking a match

a spark
during the moon eclipse
the heater turns on

best view
of the clear night moonset
by the stove

fireplace
decoration in the storm
the only warmth

in the half-light
the furnace kicks in
solar eclipse

lifting the sun
over morning mountains
frosty woodsmoke

moving closer
to the woodstove
the moonlight warms

houses
a cave of sound
and then the rainstorm
leaves the roof

a chain of old keys
in a closed house
unlocking memories

a tornado
just bouncing along
the mobile home

autumn
even the sun comes
to the south porch

autumn dusk
my neighbor's light
stays dark

autumn wind still
not finding a house
to rent

below stone steps
the moon has fallen
into a puddle

bodies buried
and now the house belongs
to someone else

closing the window
the fear of the unknown
in biceps

cold window
the dark moon
freezes time

in the rain
a house of sound
warm and dry

money
coming to an old house
young girls

moonset
now the room
is really cold

newly painted
the white porch turns blue
solar eclipse

seaside village
as the full moon disappears
windows light up

September west wind
the buoy bell fills the house
with clarity

the house
where I no longer live
best for moon viewing

turning out the light
then it fills the room
the moon

waiting for someone
a vacant house faces the town
in autumn

west wind
the buoy bell fills the house
with a cleaness

window
to my childhood days
mom's house

window to window
the moon moves closer
to the sea

journeys
a chain of light
rounds the mountain
train whistle

a day
wading in the river tonight
my hair is white

autumn journey
the miles disappear
into raindrops

country store
by the smell of garden tools
old-fashioned mums

jury duty
the Ukiah Valley lies
in darkness

more rain
lunch in the parking lot
at the restaurant

sunrise
climbing the mountain
with my feet

the moon sets
into the darkness
a car passes

train leaving
in the last station
footsteps

train whistle
moonlight on the trestle
gone in a roar

the way they walk
through the parking lot
strangers

kites
a night of ghosts
bumping in bare branches
the lost kite

reminding the dead
a sky blue kite carried aloft
with our names

music
balls of felt
the light malleable
in his hands

blurred circles
the flying mallets
sounded sounds

a blur
the flying mallets find
the lost sound

colored lights
the big bass turns them
golden

fingers flying
over black and white keys
the blue lights

fresh tonight
those old songs
spirit written

history
in the wine glass
all that jazz

island music
at sunset the coolness
in the high notes

notes
coming together
in smiles

without sticks
the performers drumming
on their thighs

neighbors
coming darkness
all my neighbors leave
distant lights

feuding neighbors
his dogs bark
at my thistles

jays taking over
the too sunny porch
a noisy neighbor

painting
a painter's brush
in the autumn scene
yellow cottonwoods

coming closer
a perfectly round moon
sometimes I get it right

photography
a picture
to photograph
a laugh

jump!
and the shutter clicks
out of step

out of focus
in the camera's lens
a new face

photographing the moon
only the filter makes it
red

reflection pool
on the faces of the crowd
common tears

shoulder-elbow
the contest to shape
a boob

politics

earth
shadowing the moon
our wars

lunar eclipse
debates about corporeal
punishment

protesting
high energy prices
my altar candle

talk of war
the diminishing moon
glows red

the riot's scar
on the black pillar
more cold

recycling

Central Park pond
recycled by dark waves
moon shapes

junk
recycled
junk

religion

autumn tides
sacrificial straw dolls
following the gods

autumn
the shrine roof reappears
in the blue sky

made of cement
the Statue of Liberty
our goddess

wish coins
sinking into the fountain
the moon

scarecrow

bewitched
the tattered scarecrow
in autumn wind

midnight trembling
where knees would be
scarecrow

tattered clothes
the ghost of scarecrow
moves the wind

unable to paint
her garden scarecrow becomes
an art form

school
children
waiting for the school bus
the sun comes first

college class
the seeing-eye dog
closes his

free English
for the college football season
only cheers

school kids
tossing sticks from a bridge
autumn leaves

school play
the frog princess wallops
the boys at recess

high school life class
the snickers reading
everyone's mind

shopping
yard sale goods
the junk looking better
to the collector

estate sale
the unworked walnut boards
brings the highest bid

sleep
curled sleep
unwinding rapidly
nightmare

late risers
will they miss
the moon?

one sleeps
and one watches
moon set

the roar of rain
a substitute for sleep
at three a. m.

yawning
the need for sleep returns
with the storm's end

wounds and injuries
after a storm
of three children on the beach
one limps

all of the sound
from the mute's fingers
bells

ballet lessons
nearly forgotten
by bent feet

burning leaves
in my palm the warmth
of a blister

chemotherapy
history falls away
with the hair

divorced
again she postpones
scattering his ashes

last glimpse
of the slender moon
approaching blindness

leaning
grass grows into autumn
I walk with a stick

on my toe
moon-viewing pain
the broken blister

pain corner
the vet and dentist
share a house

nightfall
and now I am wearing
a cast

nightfall
I cannot remember what I did
all day

plastic
my leg numb
in the cast

writing
a new shorthand
poems written in the dark
of the moon

at the end
the red excitement
of poetry

blurry computer
still wearing the glasses
that watched the moon

chasing the moon
with paper and pen
still it disappears

dust covered brushes
in the autumn storm
ink flows

harvest moon
picking the poems
for an anthology

harvest moon
still not enough poems
for a book

faking it
the patterns of a life script
shadows on frost

first light
scribbled moon poems
stay on the line

moon poems
written with old light
merely a reflection

moonset
the days I didn't keep
a journal

moon silver
wobbling in my hand
pencil shine

pencil
the color of trees
wet with rain

pull of the tides
the poet writes one more poem
at moonset

so full
the moon brightens the room
with poems

warmer now
the page fills
with ink

watching the moon set
the carpenters coming to work
and a poet

words end when
a book blows away
thoughts begin

writing words down
and then it is gone
a morning moon

writing
for the wrong reasons
competition

FALL Animals

animals
strange smell
listening to outdoor music
an unseen animal

bats
before the concert
the arrival of the conductor
bats

blacker night
stars going out
in bat wings

full moon set
satisfied the bats go
back into hiding

outdoor concert
unfolding the music
bats

birds
birds fly by
the faded moon
morning

buying a ticket
for a flight south
birds already gone

distance
a bird vanishes before
it gets there

moon not yet set
a crow flies over it
to get warm

robber birds
their nests picked clean
by fall

sea winds
flying birds walk through
the grass

bugs and worms
monster bug
creeping over the grass
tree shadow

squashing a bug
how the will to live
wiggles his legs

the mess loggers leave
mosses and bug mouths
make it magic again

crossing the road
fish worms following
the original stream

butterfly
a falling leaf
up from the earth
a matching butterfly

migrating
monarchs stop on the beach
wait for the haiku

migrating
yet the monarch takes time
to visit me

white butterfly
afternoon sunshine
slides away

cat
a lost cat
each moving shadow takes
on his shape

autumn
leaping into my lap
the brown cat

autumn
meeting on the cat
flea and wood tick

brown and gold
autumn disappears in the grass
with the brindle cat

chalk
the smell of a cat
sun-warmed

discord
the music between
cat and dog

full moon
jumping on my lap
a wide-eyed cat

full moon
the cat too squats
to stare

harvest time
the cat brings me
another mouse

late afternoon
the cat tries to tell me
with a meow

leaping
out of autumn leaves
the ginger cat

moon haiku
the cat plays with
a fake mouse

moon watching
the cat comes in
on cold feet

moon watching
the cat's sleep
in the poem

night reduced
to a rush of rain
a purring cat

no fire
the warmth of a yellow cat
behind the stove

no passing
the dead cat lies
on the yellow line

scanning the porch
the watch cat looks for
the already-set moon

storm barometer
the cat's bushy tail
standing up straight

the cat growls
at the close moon
invader

the cat meows
his favorite chair
taken by moonlight

the radiance
of the dark cat
full moon

watching the cat's eyes
watching me
watching the night

cicada
cicada cry
on the day my son
left home

cicada husk
filled with warmth again
at sunset

cicada voices
bridging the field
with coolness

project complete
but left on my desk
a cicada husk

the crippled child
why the cicada husk
is perfect
cricket
a ceramic chicken
not eating my pets
the crickets

crickets
echoing crickets
sky grass gold

crickets
in the autumn grass
voice of the dead

nothing to see
in the dark of the moon
crickets' drone

slowing
the early morning light
one cricket

so cricket
what do you take
for insomnia?

the odds
of surviving autumn
cricket chirp

crows
a crow caws
the river bends
in the distance

a crow caws
the low river moves
closer to autumn

black on black
crows copulating
on asphalt

concert
by the Kronos quintet
a crow too

crows mate again
as if they are bored
with the long day

crow's cawing
the shape of his shadow
scrapes the cliff

flutes
echoing each other
two crows

on the switchback
a pair of crows
fornicating

outdoors
listening to the concert
a crow

the crow
brings to the frozen limb
more cold

the crow's sandwich
a piece of old bread
covered with ants

roast chicken aroma
guess who is coming to dinner
two crows

two crows
hide behind the buckwheat
sharing a waffle

yesterday's rain
the crow shinier now
in sunshine

deer

coyote bushes
turning into the moon
two deer

full moon
clang of the buoy bell shows
the deer's dark shape

moonset
coming from the bushes
a pair of deer

screeching brakes
the doe heads into the woods
and back out again

showing the way
for the mountain road
a stag's voice

steam rising
from the gutted deer
still alive

water's edge
a deer is drinking
in the darkness

dogs

beggar's alley
an abandoned dog asks
everyone for love

hoar frost
on his muzzle now
on his grave

long-haired lady
both her dogs have
bobbed tails

doves
autumn air
the mourning dove lands
very close

dragonfly
the dragonfly
on mother's gravestone
something of her

ducks
lifting the calm
sea with a flap of wings
the duck

the duck's wake
attended by two old crows
and some ants

feathers
a feather falls
reading something
in the wind

frogs
from the trees
into the pond a frog
and leaves

finches
thistledown flying
with a spot of sun
gold finches

flies
beach meditation
complete with the cold
the fly's feet

geese
a vee of geese
and a Volkswagen
leaving town

tied together
the skein of geese
patch the sky

grasshopper
the row of ants
a grasshopper crosses the path
headless

gulls
flying away
as if it's the sea's error
the gray gull

in the fog
ghosts by the cliffs
change into gulls

sunset
pointing where he was
gull tracks

sunset
with the last flight of gulls
the warmth is gone

hawks
looking here & there
wind moves the hawk's body
over a mouse hole

insects
in farewell
insects chirp in grasses
our lips dry

jays
rusty hinge
opening the garden gate
the jay's cry

mice
no cheese
the mouse nibbles
a small book

visitors leaving
me alone in the gallery
the errant mouse

migrating birds
braided air
migrating birds
pass me by

cloud feathers
rearranging the sky
migrating birds

moths
outdoor concert
drawn to the light music
moths

later
coming to the concert
more moths

trapped
in the spider web I tear
the moth flies

owls
owls
a mountain of darkness
split by the screams

night
sliding down the hill
the owl's cry

snowy owl
turns his head – there
the quarter moon

pets
a lost pet
each moving shadow takes
on its shape

raccoons
eating leftovers
in my relationship corner
bandit-faced raccoons

ravens
nevermore
the raven approaches
the lone man

salmon
a leaping salmon
the moon sets red
in the blue sea

seals
foggy morning
the sleeping of the seals
is not to be seen

215

full moon
sleeping on a rock
shine of wet seals

into the opening
harbor seals bring
moonlight

moonset
harbor seals
coming home

sea lions
cry of sea lions
lost in the mist
all those years

scorpion
garden sundial
the scorpion marks
autumn hours

sheep
gazing alone
out to sea
one sheep

silkworm
silk-lined coffin
yet no one grieves when
the silkworm spins

snails
harvest moon
shiny kelp beds full
of snails

sparrows
just ripe
the whole sparrow family
in my grapes

spider
after dusting
the spiders seem at home
everywhere

a spider's web
hanging in the wind chime
sunset colors

wind trapped
released from spider webs
it sways

swallows
swarm of swallows
netting in the sky
sunbeams

toad
so earth-like
yet the toad's belly
a small moon

FALL Plants

bamboo

a gesture
of a slanted bamboo
in my hand

bamboo flute
finding the song
in fingers

bamboo flute
the notes come out
round and rooted

bamboo in autumn
the view to the east
completely green

teaching
bamboo to sing
breath

bracken

autumn arrives
first in the bracken stems
brown

bushes

a barking dog
in the morning light
only a bush

blackberry sun
dark places by the river
in jam jars

butterfly bush
winged they fly away
as seeds

cacti

purple
leaking from the shadows
cactus

dead plants

blowing not blowing
the wisdom of a dried leaf
rests on the ground

giving up
the dried plant's leaf
smell of water

driftwood

driftwood
sweater gray in
brown tones

fields

whiter
a full moon above
cotton fields

flowers

autumn
flowers of farewell
without fragrance

chrysanthemums
cupped in my hands
spilling water

daisies gone
counting votes with a mum
Bush, Gore, Bush, Gore. . .

dandelion seeds
the deeds of which
I am ashamed

growing wild
in front of the church
naked ladies*

*autumn amaryllis

lining walks
in the monks' garden
cockscomb

many colors
yet the mum's smell
of autumn

moonset
the daisies nod
in a deep bow

nodding to daisies
I miss the bus but not
the wind

rose scent thin
rising from old thickets
faded flowers

school bus stop
anxious faces of children
black-eyed susans

swollen hands
unfolding after prayer
chrysanthemums

the new moon
curving light on the petals
of a chrysanthemum

tit for tat
thorn-full of skin
pruning roses

to grow old gracefully
the white parachute dance
of the dandelion

who's old now?
the mums open whitely
under a new moon

heavy with wings
of the green warblers
withered sunflowers

fruits

apricots
late in autumn the sun
enters my mouth

berry colors
as kids we wore them
on our lips

falling to the ground
the sound of the full moon
apples

first grapes
the rising sun in rows
of rosy clusters

leafless
yet the tree has gathered
persimmons

married for wisdom
only years later did I know
the sweetness of plums

not ripe
black grapes in the fields
after the fire

pale fog
yellow vineyards over
champagne cellars

stolen fruit
pear juice sticks
to our fingers

the stars
in the apple's center
seed distance

youth
once grapes hung
on this vine

grains
wheat harvested
now for a cake for the winter
birthday

coming to earth
the color of ripe grain
in the moon

harvest time
the golden grain color
in the moon

not yet ripe
rice in the fields
of the dead one

rice
and for my husband
2 - 3 more chestnuts

my teeth
entering a wheat field
harvest

grass
10-minute parking
the pampas grass waves
good-bye

dry humor
not even grass grows
over his grave

ochre earth
bent by the wind
dried grass

purple grasses
the sunsets into
its familiar

such green
in the autumn lawn
sewer system

sunrise gilds
a harvest moon
golden grasses

a hillside
the ochre earth
in dried grass

leaves
autumn color
in a heap of leaves
fire

autumn wind
bringing brightness
to the leaves

autumn wind
someone walks in the leaves
with red and gold

bridge
across the narrow creek
fallen leaves

falling leaves
last night's dream
forgotten

forest path
leaves getting higher
as they fall

glistening red
frost-glazed maple leaves
bright blossoms

holding the heat
a cut of sunshine
in the dried leaf

it's autumn
even the moon thins
when leaves fall

leaves blowing
the crackle of fire
without warmth

leaves falling
I find no one else
in the cemetery

leaves
hearing autumn
fall

leaves
leaving
leaf colors

rippling
over stones in a ditch
dried leaves

Saturday cleaning
the tree drops
another leaf

shooting star
moonlight glints on the dew
of a falling leaf

still rippling
leaves on the stream
when they fall

taking the path
falling leaves hide
its going

the last leaf
holding on
to a dew drop

the shadow
of someone with wings
ivy leaves

mold
penetrating
the memory of parents
that moldy smell

moss
alive again
on the gravestone of a friend
moss

granite stone
moss filling the cracks
with a name

Spanish moss
the shape of melancholy
in the trees

mushrooms
drawing
a drawing
mushroom

first rain
marking the calendar
for mushrooms

mushrooms
moving up and down
cellar stairs

mushroom hunting
the wild cry of a bird
still hidden

showing the way
for the mountain path
mushrooms

treasures
arising from the rain
mushrooms

pines
an old moon
pine trees hide
its final descent

cast to earth
a woman picks it up
pine tree womb

darkness moving
moon radiance on the sea
shore pines

fog clearing
among the pines
sunny maples

lifting the sky
the pine bough
as if in a wind

moonset
on a path through pines
silver seas

moving north
the moon's fluid path
shines in the pines

pine wind
beyond the shore
moon set

the shape
of shore pines
a cool wind

waiting on the bench
cushions of pine needles
my nervous butt

seeds
designed for planting
the dagger-shaped seed
stuck on my dress

trees
a painter's brush
in the autumn scene
yellow cottonwoods

autumn trees
the only green is in
the lost kite

birdsong still
in the shape of
a fallen tree

changing the trees
in the night someone
with a flashlight

fog clearing
leaves on the maple
nearly bare

golden autumn
by the koi pond
liquid ambers

gray to gold
in the fog the trees
turn to autumn

native oaks
still have leaves
and the moon

on the stage
redwood needles
flute music

outer space
limbs of the bare oak reach
the farthest stars

redwood stump
another atheist left
in the forest

river light
slanting into afternoon
redwood trees

smoky haze
in the golden trees
an autumn drizzle

stop sign
along the road to winter
red sumac

the candle trees
stain the autumn skies
a flame

the tree
its memories still
in its bark

trees still
listening to the flute
low notes

twinkling lights
the aspen touched
by the all-seen

what do they think
redwoods hearing music
from a shakuhachi

vegetables
morning after
the pepper rubbed red
by the storm

pumpkin yellow
over ripe fields
the harvest moon

pumpkins
full of their own praise
in pies

roadside stand
to the crooked pumpkin
I give a grin

vines
red
autumn in the creeper
vines

weeds
a puff of wind
the field of thistles
grows larger

golden straw bales
connected to the field by
small yellow flowers

growing golden
the moon sets above
marijuana plants

prickly and yet
how gently dew is held
dried thistle

redder
autumn's poison ivy
touched by the sun

touch me
my leaves are so pretty
poison ivy

WINTER

WINTER Moods

angry

in anger
striking with the whip
silence

still mad
he sends cut flowers
with thorns

anxious

anxious
the cypress in a night wind
cracks its branches

climbing the walls
along the coast crashes
the heavy surf

night wind
the sound of things
I fear

porch lights on
the snowing snow
make us nervous

tension
in the daughter's voice
Okay

being alone

alone in the fog
yet never truly alone
one rock

more visitors?
just the start-up noise
of a copy machine

my solitude
infusing the winter
with space

no moon
now the room
is really cold

the rattle of
chocolate wrappers
alone

being silent

deep silence
it takes the shape
of the inner ear

silence
between words
stories

silence
drawing together lovers
a silver cord

silence
between objects known
others becoming

silence
fingers pointing
forwards

silence
its size shaped
by loneliness

227

silence
of an aside glance
darts

silence
the stone in your mouth
is a tongue

silence
the nothingness of something
takes a name

silence
the width of an echo
forgotten

silence
when naked and alone
a tunnel

boredom
boredom
on the third day without power
peeling nail polish

boredom
stained by watercolors
afternoon

bored with winter
a beach walk finds
abandoned toys

endless cups of tea
and still
the rain comes down

local radio
even the jazz is now
country music

manifesting
the afternoon
in yawns

spreading around
in the doctor's waiting room
yawns

weighted waiting
the doctor's scales show
more pounds

coping
a glass of water
in me another
clear thought

a leaking pipe
she calls again to ask
if I forgot

another storm
the welcomed activity
of building a fire

charming me
my charming smile
for visitors

even shorter
on the magic slate
haiku

in the lingerie catalog
younger than my daughter
my new image

the librarian
bends over the book
Dancing Made Easy

the narrow path
my two feet walk
another religion

writing haiku
the art of being busy
on Sunday

depressed
dark days
seeing deep in a flower
my lack of beauty

depressed
watching my broken toe
turn blue

silence
heavy with the thought
I don't care

embarrassment
virgin snow he says
her cheeks redden
with the cold

ephemeral
dreaming
the things as seen
by the moon

drifting fog
it passes so quickly
this life

a bird's flight
and then I am gone
and forgotten

fears
banging on mirrors
the eclipsed moon hears
and comes back

fearing death
even when famous
snow on iris

the moon wanes
with it fear grows
in darkness

forgetting
cinders
forgotten
thoughts

guilt
the high wall of
a mother's disapproval
silence

happiness
bamboo
the sincerity of clearness
in the painting

reading the light
before the rock
a bowed spirit

helpless
batteries low
still humming the inane tune
from the newscast

storm over
and still
no power

winter décor
odd candles ringed
by wax splatters

jealous
jealous
she recommends cat's claw
for my health

the jealous sound
of the neighbor's generator
outage outrage

winter thaw
the rich man's terrace
racing downhill

love
a pair reunited
in their love of jazz
blues

a triangle
of village love and lust
a couple splits

concert applause
she kisses her husband
on the cheek

in winter
from such a face
mother love

needs
night wind
the need to talk to someone
who listens

pursing lips
the old lady wants to love
the trumpet player

suspected thief
I only wanted to see moonlight
on the blooming plum

peaceful
healing
the quiet of the sea
after the boat

visiting monks
ah! the desert peace
of the web site

wind-blown
she gives in after
the storm

praise
overcast morning
yet the world comes up
to my praise

recovering
a slice of skin
the time it takes to feel
broken glass

healing
after each wave
the smooth sea

in a fever
falling asleep on a book
that opens to a dream

recovering
seaside landscape
bedside escape

the wake of a boat
my thread of thought
on the mend

touching the zit
such a little pain
enlivens the day

relief
first relief
in the outdoor privy
the wind chimes

bowel movement
bringing my offering of earth
back to earth

remembering
fifty years later
that child born again
winter moonset
-for Heidi

taking up the brush
the day of that teacher
enters my hand

second story
watching the boy with a
snowball
and his victim

revenge
two aunts
discussing family traits
one is always wrong

ribbons
of trees marked for harvest
in my pocket

the dream
of killing the neighbor's dog
my cat dead

scared
no power
is okay but we're scared
with the phone out

sleep
sleepy
the setting moon covered
with clouds

unable to sleep
one by one stars fall
into the sea

thankful
earth
bringing my offering of earth
back to earth

getting older
how to thank the one
who built this bench

in winter storm
seaweed tied in knots
we stick together

thinking

a woman's
sleeping face
fantasy

footprint
of an idea
underwater

I see
a new understanding
of my blind friend

tranquility
a bird vanishes
with it

wishes

desire to sleep
the full moon covered
by warm clouds

safety tested
doctor's office scales
off by pounds

snowstorm
the desire for ice cream
sends us into it

wishes
as if I could will it
to keep snowing

WINTER Occasions
*Note all the holiday haiku
are in New Year section.*

beginning of winter
winter begins
the exalted visitor
from high peaks

winter arrives
in the early darkness
solitude

end of winter
all the ice
on the pond no longer fits
end of winter

Ground Hog Day
tradition
the meat at dinner
is hamburger

believing
in the myth
adults

St. Brigit's Day
St. Brigit's Day
this year only three women
celebrate

St. Valentine's Day
his and her
2003 Valentine's gifts
gas masks

in a game of cards
so many red hearts
Valentine's Day

St. Valentine's Day
a chance to send love
to perfect strangers

Valentine's Day
my maiden aunt calls
collect

Valentine's Day
rid of him I find
wind and rain

weddings
wedding chapel
thrown rice falls
on icy steps

WINTER Celestial

cloud

cirrus clouds
a net is cast
into the lake

cloud cover
the shadow of hours
still passes

snow-covered hills
the line of white
clouds

cold

colder now
the night lengthens
with more frost

colder now
the puzzle of snow
in salt crystals

cold flat seas
the weight of winter crosses
the water

such cold
the sere grass shakes
a slender shadow

the coming day
pushes before it
more cold

hailstones

day moon
suddenly on the ground
hailstones

hail
on the lute strings
stiff fingers

silence
after the hailstorm
colder

somewhere high
a game played by young gods
hailstones

winter
coming to earth
a hailstone

ice

ice breaking up
in the greenhouse
a bud opens

icicle melting
its shape in the snow
a flower

an icicle drips
its shape deepens
in the snow

the icicle drips
its shape again
deep in snow

mist

coastal fog
the very wet brush
of Chinese paintings

freezing fog
where are all the people
who hurt me

shoreline fog
unrolling the day
the north wind

white mist
the oldest visitor
at the seashore

moon
a crooked moon
one day lacking
in its shape

bright enough
to write a poem
the cold moon

cold moon
the bell of evening skies
ring blue

moon-pulled sea
water to unstring
our bounds

night nurse
going from room to room
the moon

reading old diaries
the cloudy moon is
a bit dusty

sparkling branches
of the crooked shore pine
a cold moon

the moon sinks
into the freezing seas
a silver path

rain
first winter rain
something in me swells
with rejoicing

freezing rain
on the plank bridge
smooth timber

rain
filling the dry room
with its roar

rainbow
seven parts
connected to legs
a rainbow

silence
in a rain shower
seven colors

sky
clear skies
sucked into the void
litigation

overcast skies
on the great red lantern
sunlight

such a day
the sky lets down
snowflakes

snow

big flakes
California-sized
5 minute storm

blossom hill
shining like the sun
snow flowers

bright snow
the day is shortened
by that much

deep snow
the glacier returns
to Yosemite

fallen arches
from great white clouds
snow drifts

falling too
the space around each flake
soft and downy

first snow
surprised the cold
can burn

first snowfall
repeating the presence
of tall trees

heavy snow
in all the brightness
something dark

layer of snow
on the scarecrow's coat
does it warm him?

foreign language
reflected from the mirror
sun on snow

for my book
snowflakes seem to be
blessings

melting the snow
last year's rubbish
new

my white flakes
in the neighbor's yard
a smaller gray

raindrops
or melting snow
both are fine

rocks in a garden
the first to appear
in melting snow

rounding out
half-dome peak
snow clouds

snow
on the child's tongue
a cry of delight

snowdrift
the sun climbs into it
flake by flake

snowfall
from the dark ground
again the light

snowing again
in the winter night
a drift of stars

snowstorm
the white cat comes in
whiter

something growing
in the deserted garden
snow deepens

tracks in light snow
her shoes leaving the sign
of feminine parts

white flowers
blooming in the window
snowflakes

winter sun
low across snow drifts
cold starlight

stars

a few flakes
still falling
stars

power outage
turns up the wattage
of the stars

power protest
the brightness of stars
makes us bold

silence
the dust of stars'
shining radiance

stars
guardian angels are
everywhere

stardust
the shining radiance of
silence

soul bathing
in hot springs
desert stars

won by one
the sea turns
into stars

storm

sea storm
iron howling hollow
in the bell buoy

sky rain white
only waves come ashore
during the storm

sun on crashing waves
someone's storm is
somewhere else

the arrow points
in another direction
after the storm

winter storm
slippery when wet sign
slides down the hill

sun

afternoon music
spreads across the room
bars of sunlight

frosty earth
sun comes in brilliant
fire flames

a southern sun
and now the whales
pass us by

Sunday afternoon
the lowered sun moves
into the art center

sunset
arriving in Point Arena
the beat generation

winter sun
gentled by the long journey
deep in my bones

winter sun
the color of stone
a cold wind

winter sunrise
the dream of a sheep
spins a cover

wind

gliding gulls
the wind-blown beach
smoother now

high winds
a cloud turns in
its silence

in the sea mists
closer to mysteries
just wind

WINTER Terrestrial

avalanche
stone chimes
after the snow fall
avalanche

beach
a letter mailed
already waves from Japan
high on the beach

the beach is clean
with new driftwood
winter storms

the cold wind
now part of the day
at the beach

winter beach
widened by the tide
and a lone gull

desert
cold desert
stretched to the horizon
silence

earthquake
earthquake
the lab slips
on the floor

falls
water over ice
the falls slow
to a trickle

fields
even when empty
the scarecrow guards
fenceless fields

glacier
silence
snow freezes the movement
into a glacier

hills
in sunny California
we head for the hills
snowstorm

island
all roads closed
our mountain hamlet
an island

lake
darkness
a presence in a dream
of a frozen lake

glass lake
the reach of space
in the cold

on the lake
the smooth water
frozen

overcast
the clouds frozen
in the lake

snow mountains
hidden in the white sky
a sealed lake

land's end

as land's end
is crumbling into the sea
far mountains in fog

land crumbling
into kelp-covered rocks
distant mountains

land's end
the fog covers one rock
with moss

mountains

a new day
snow softens the mountain
with color

ashes
on the far mountain
snow

craggy mountain
even the young ones
look old

frozen in the rain
a waterfall of earth
mountain slide

last shalom
down the ski slope
sunset rays

mountain
at the very top
it is gone

morning cold
is that snow on the mountain
or a drift of fog

mountain pass
snow I thought had melted
among the trees

mountain slopes
my rain
into your snow

winter mud
the mountain moves
down the road

paths

the path
deeper into winter
deep in snow

mountain masters
with more than wisdom
the narrow path

pond

frozen pond
a woman speaks with her
hand
before her mouth

puddle

in a puddle
his goodbye disappears
snowman

river

as snow melts
the ground whitens
see the water

ice
a river smoothing
each rock

rain stops
leaving in the winter creek
its roar

roads
downhill
the winter creek
our road

road salt
the line of frost
that lingers

rocks
as if a tree
could be a rock
in its roundness

hot springs
cool in the river
a jasper stone

old friends
how different in winter rain
are the rocks

rocks
drawing themselves
closer to water

rocks
giving and taking
the colors

time
waiting for a picture
the unfinished rock

seas
a tranquil wind
in a stone house
fossil sand

at sea
guardian angels are
everywhere

fog rolling in
the sea welcomes home
all our water shapes

huge waves
rolling over the coast
another storm

mountains
their snow-capped shape
in each wave

ocean blue
the twist of veins
in a wrist

out of the blue
the next storm comes in
from the sea

reunion
cold sea water shakes
my hand

seaside
bedside
visitor

silence
between crashing waves
the briefness of foam

storm morning
the sea takes up the light
in broken waves

sunset
snow-melt river cools
the sea

wave shapes
mountains and valleys
of the sea

wills
invisible bending
just the sea

shore
huge waves
rolling over the coast
storm shores

shoreline
a black ink painting
of far mountains

winter storms
Stillwater Cove
isn't

tide
riptide
in the sea the pull of
silence

silence
in the sea the pull
of riptide

valley
spring light
the snow-melt stream
flows to the valley

volcano
smoking a little
snow on the top
of a volcano

WINTER Livelihood

art

a binge
and two aspirins
poems arrive

Art in the Redwoods
people showing people
redwood art

artist's diet
how lovingly she sketches
the sandwich

art show voices
in my head disagreeing
with the judges

a story told
the tapestry fades into
silence

bamboo brushes
the sincerity of clearness
in the painting

bodega bags
the artist's model
thinks thirst

body parts
hidden in a pencil
growing larger

buying a pencil
the obligation to draw
a good picture

cross-section
the view beyond
another world

faraway flute
painting on the theater wall
the bamboo

first
artist
water

frog knees
they never seem to please
no matter how I draw them

gallery sitting
redwoods in the window
the biggest visitors

ink
following the pen
idle thoughts

long-time supporters
at Gualala Arts Center
a group of redwoods

looking at art
not looking at art
the cleaning lady

oil paints
and the visitors
with sweaty feet

opening her door
the sight of clay tools
touches my palm

out of the gallery
which ceramic piece
sticks in my mind?

painting
with pigments
rock colors

passing a studio
a whiff of clay dust
draws me in

patchwork quilt
if I could find a pattern
to my jumbled days

picture stories
rolled into a dizziness
a scroll book

pit firing
the best design
on the cracked pot

pots so hot
the whiteness of smoke
burns black

redwood fragrance
the art on the walls
rises a notch

rocks
abstract artists
with water

seeing the door
the clay on your hands
awakens my past

seventh drawing
beginning to feel I own
the sunflowers

snow print
the very few lines
in the sumi-e

stained glass
by that artist woman
who sins

still water
splashing a rock
in the painting

Sunday afternoon
only locals in the gallery
breathing deeply

the many hours
together with pounds of clay
blue shadows

the prize
in the art show
not getting it

watching strangers
admire my sculpture
with grins

watercolor
of the seascape
paper too wet

wet clay
the potter dries her hands
over the pit fire

Basho translations
a break
from translating Basho
my own poem

Basho's birthplace
the memory of him
in clear wind

Basho's death
no trace of dust
on his poems

more haiku
typing up Basho's
then mine

cleaning
after the bath
the exciting shivers
of clean clothes

another rainy day
cleaning out of the toaster
more crumbs

bird eaten by a bird
I write a check to pay
the garbage collector

thaw weather
still a bit of shaving crème
by his ear

winter nights
going to bed with Orion
my teeth brushed

winter storm
washing our dinner plates
left outside

underarm deodorant
outlines her feet perfectly
powder on the rug

clothes
clothes line
heavy with ice airing
death garments

cold
on a winter beach
gum boots

festival clothes
for today's trip to Fuji
snow-covered slopes

into the cold
letting the sleep
out of my braid

jury duty
I can't decide
what to wear

personal lawsuit
behind the barbed wire
the orange suit

personalities
in pairs on the floor
shoes

socks
she snickers to say
toe mittens

straight hair
yet it curls around my finger
being braided

taking off
one of the sweaters
between storms

the cold season
hair combed wide
blue sparks

threadbare warmth
of an old nightly
end of winter

winter
naked trees against a grey sky
my new wool suit

concerts
announcing
the song *Future Floors*
forgotten

a nod
the progression changes
a beat

applause
the music belongs
to the stars

applause
the music returns to
the performers

a shiver of keys
in the middle of the bar
ripples

beginning
trumpet lessons
fresh sounds

between sets
the silence of a woman
yawning

candlelight
merging spot lights
note world

clear lights
the strange music sounds
very modern

concert
the stillness outdoors
cold

draining the lizard
the trumpet player's horn
upside down

encore
the old guy's finger
in his ear

encore
the yawning stops
at the drums

flute music
under the spell
the pen stops

flagstones
music smoothes
a snowy path

glass beads
the notes of the concert
bound together

group
dancing piano finger
tips

harmonizing
before the concert
snowflakes

instrumental sigh
part of the composition
audience noise

intermission
the modern music turns to
neighbors' voices

jazz musicians
following the notes
to the concert's end

jazz musicians
wives selling the disks
on a wobbly table

late evening
complex sounds combine
with tiredness

many lands
coming forth here
from a violin

modern composition
electric banjo bass and
a sneeze

modern music
audience noise
reinvented

modern music
a slit in the curtain
more unknown

music rocking
yet not one sleeps
this late

one coast
to another
fusion music

one tone
in the shakuhachi holding
our breath

on the guitar
bending the note
a blue light

on the stage
the many wires
of flute music

plucking
the violin string
changes colors

plugged in
the violin player
electric

pounded by feet
another instrument is
the floor

professional jazz
the writer takes out
his camera

puzzle
musicians fitting new sounds
together

rainy coast
the desert comes to us
as jazz

solo
arriving from New York
the trumpet

suspense
found again
bent note

taps
played as jazz
end the evening

the finale
at the last note
eight smiles

tired
the violinist smiles
more

trumpet notes
hanging out his
shirt tails

wiggling
and then the atonal piece
changes

dreams
curled sleep
unwinding rapidly
in a nightmare

dream-catcher
our car passes the house
of sleepers

kid's bedtime
the protest ends
with a bath

moonset
cold creeps under the blanket
in a new place

reading of dreams
to live by the sea years ago
the ocean is near

sound asleep
yet such a noise from
your snoring

storm warning
the old woman sleeps
in her snoring

trip dreams
yet in the morning
still at home

winter dreams
ice cubes floating
in a glass of water

yawning
the need for sleep returns
with the storm's end

duty
figuring the tip
he stares out the window
filling with snow

late in January
saving the old calendar
for the IRS

protesting
my energy bills
a dead battery

volunteer
watching the clock
not move

entertainment
a slow bass note
the evening slides from silence
into applause

entertainment
the unseasonable snowfall
gathers us around

four Deva kings
the empty museum
is very full

jazz
pattern in the old rug
dizzy

knitting
in between the rows
sea waves

music fills
every cell of still listeners
candle flicker

old folks
jazz cool in Point Arena
Odd Fellows Hall

museum snow
still unmarked days
after the storm

museum garden
water treasure
in a frozen pond

puzzle pieces
the table top becomes
a faraway place

rainy day
the kind of people in
the museum

waiting
for the movie to start
our many lives

food and drink
coffee machine down
everyone sleepless
yet nodding

colder now
the full moon fills
the empty tea cup

evening
the last wine glass
holds the light

grocery shelves
just what we need is
sold out

hailstones
and now the desire
for popcorn

paper food
bought and sold
dolls don't mind

penny candy
now costs a dollar
sticks to dentures

slurp swallows
from a clay nest
tea aroma

tea
a good friend with wit
and teasing

too big
the on-sale tablecloth
makes two

vegetarian
the worm in her
Caesar salad

wine glasses
fill and empty
with light

winter dawn
all the bright stars
in cookie jars

friends
dawn party
in the voltage
of spirits

my skinny friend
eats a box of Ex-lax
I finish the Oreos

new age friend
first he gives my cat
a massage

paper solitude
the pleasure carried
on a postage stamp

two women meet
their perfumes however
clash

winter day
his call from the South
filled with warmth

winter rain
doctor's waiting room full
of old friends

winter sunshine
the yellow telephone rings
with a friend's voice

funerals
an open mouth
no longer breathing
silence

blurring the star
handfuls of damp earth
tears

cemetery
populated with bodies
filled with life

graveside service
afterwards dirt clings
to my high heels

more rain
the newly-filled grave
overflowing

natural gas
the coffin becomes an ark
lighter than air

ninety pounds
her frail body held together
with hugs

no embalming
in the tribal tradition
eco-green

prayers
in a foreign language
our tears

silence
to seek and wrap around
the body nothing

winter rain
on its way to the sea
in a square hole

winter rain
over the memorial
a pink umbrella

wood
with a life of its own
resurrection

furniture

a dying man
waves from the window
clouds rush by

afternoon silence
made even louder
by a ticking

blow job
on the loveseat
carved swallows

clean sheets
moon shine covers my bed
with new dreams

deep in winter
tropical flower prints
on white pillows

frost
the moon shines on my bed
as if it's cold

silence
from a kerosene lamp
smoke pictures

the chair
too small for the cat
by a tail and a leg

wiggling feet
miles covered in waiting
in chairs

winter weaves
a pile of pillows
on a hard chair

under a rug
a thin bug moving
silence

health
a flute
played with each breath
this body

blip blip-blip-blip
scaring the machine
scaring me

clipboard
hospital status symbol
on mine are haiku

dentist's office
everything broken
seems a tooth

dentist's office
the old pine has
a broken branch

doctor's office
the rain gutter
also leaks

finding my way
behind new glasses
dewy grass

flu weather
how little I really
need to do

flu with coughing
snow in gusts of wind swirls
under the eaves

growing older
the winter fly and I
in the doctor's office

ICU
still on the machine
another's agonies

ICU
watching the machine
watching me

in surgery
who will write down
my haiku

into the MRI
I take all my images
as mine

lunch
at the doctor's office
blood sugar test

modern sculpture
in the doctor's waiting room
pelvis bone model

MRI tube
to practice death
closing the coffin

my neighbors
in the doctor's office
all new

PMS crying jag
wiping my eyes I find
the sun shining

pre-dawn
even my cane
is cold

social center
the waiting room
of the doc

tons of color
seas of water entertain
the invalid

the poem
waiting for the ambulance
lost on another road

the swan
later leg cramps force
a yoga position

turning their heads
the empty birdfeeder
comes to mind

winter injury
a year later my leg
a solid white cast

winter rain
the doctor's waiting room
full of old friends

heating
a home
the invisible heart
of wood and stone

a cutting wind
around the woodpile
a flying axe

a flicker
blazing from a match
three points of fire

brick and rust
surrounding the fire
its color

candle shadows
the night gives up
the shape of things

fire bricks
in the sarcophagus of a kiln
winter shadows

fire magic
even modern folks circle
around it

fire so hot
even the smoke
is consumed

first warmth
woodchips swept up
from the floor

meditation breath
blowing harder on the embers
to start the fire

more wood
the pit fire traded
for a pot

moving closer
to my stove the moonlight
warms

pine fire smoke
delight in the smell of
another's warmth

speaking in tongues
the roar of the fire
in flickering

sunset
a fire burns into the sea
the kiln cools

warm by the stove
crunch of snow shoveling
butters my toast

whispers
in the burning log
tongues of flame

winter clutter
the room is warmer
in candlelight

housing
a cave of sound
and then the rainstorm
leaves the roof

crowded room
how different men and women
stand by the walls

distance
filling the window
with stars

eaves dripping
the candle flame
flickers

housewarming
the gypsy brings a chain
of sea shells

icicles point
where no one is
inn porch

midnight room
rays of candlelight
star-cold

night window
rain taps as I play the flute
in a lower key

pointing at sunset
the corners of the house
leak in the rain

privacy fence
a job for many nails
with no results

rain
branches falling
on the roof

rain gusts
the electricity goes
on and off

sea wind
voices in cedar shingles
neighbors

sky lake cold
pours into the window
sea fog

still alive
in knotty pine walls
dragon eyes

unheated cold
at least my attic affords
a raccoon's birthplace

walls
holding up the candle light
and dark holes

inauguration sequence
inauguration
who blesses this nation
with sunshine?

cheers
first TV shot of the crowds
real pride

the crowds
in every one
a heart

crowd views
our joker asks
where's Waldo?

flags waving
over white cars
goose bumps

watching
just the motorcade
first tears

trumpet calls
drum rolls of shiver
dignitaries

old politicians
how they have aged
our gray heads

toe-tapping music
the TV picture flickers
in all colors

Chaney
in a wheelchair
jokes

biggest boos
Chaney on the TV screen
seems to hear us

Bush appears
Give him the hook!
in our room

next to Bush
the photographer cannot
point

Bush and Obama
walking side by side
twilight of an era

first cheers
Bill and Hillary Clinton
in the golden hall

times millions
a flash of colors
applause

reflection pool
on the faces of the crowd
common tears

our grandmotherly *ohs*
comments on Obama's
children

my first view
of Michele's great dress
sunshine

Capitol steps
heads of our nation
in rows

handshake
Michele wipes hers on her coat
after meeting Bush

flying
the flag flaps in cold air
with our tears

before the first note
Aretha Franklin sings
her great hat

oath of office
for vice president
all stand

steadying
his trembling hand
the old Bible

words in the roar
Chaney's gone, he's gone
fresh air

Izak Perlman
the performance only slows
the advance of meal time

classical music
everyone takes an intermission
for scrambled eggs

Obama
the crowds chant
for two years

waves of pink
cold hands held up to Obama
his severe face

lines
around his tense lips
his people

the judge stutters
the oath breaks up in
Obama's smile

stumbling tongue
the about to be President says
so help me God

President's words
our perilous times
sweetened with cake

they will be met
hope over fear
cheers

end of petty games
the time has come for us
to cheer

remake America
cheers on one coast
and then others

Hillary stares
at the back of Michele's
stern face

forceful
words of hope
murmurs yes

clapping hands
at President Obama's words
prayerful

sun
shining gold on his chest
a tiny flag

cheers
for the new President
surf on the shore

who we are
how far we have come
sacred oath

takeover
the halls of the Capitol
44th President

blessings on Obama
he raises his head
in prayer

hinge point
in history cheers
within the prayer

in prayer
flying over the crowd
pigeons

rising waves
prayer for the new President
the Pacific ocean

prayer
in the amen's
poetry

Obama's walk
already the weight
on his shoulders

cheers
Chaney leaves
with sirens

into the heavens
Bush leaves the scene
by helicopter

Biden's wife Jill
outstretched arms gather
new heads of state

raising
the Star Spangled Banner
our toasts

crowds leaving
on the Washington Mall
their smiles

misty lights
the breath of millions
halo streetlamps

ceremonies over
the sun is gone into
misty breath

lights on
in the halls of government
a golden glow

first phone call
champagne corks pop
in the new era

jury duty
a day in court
more cold seeps
into the room

boxed in
in the jury box
wanting release

courthouse community
meeting the carpenter
who cheated us

courthouse computer
it prints – again – finally
nonsense

court room
the old-book smell
of everyone

everyone waiting
for one everyone
waiting

getting acquainted
strangers cheek by jowl
in a box

jury duty
I have picked the wrong
thing to wear

jury duty
the whole town is
in the dark

lights on
I liked the courthouse better
in the dark

shuffling papers
no one moves
in the coffee smell

the school teacher
her voice carries
across the room

waiting room
again the boredom
six feet deep

waiting
everyone looks like
like cattle

words in my ears
of foreign-word tongues
jury – guilty

occupations
a crisp bill
on the vagrant's hand
dirty nails

bad business year
the publisher buys steel
bookshelves

binding books
the aroma of paste
winter solitude

blessing the day
he crumbles bread
for the birds

cold winter sunshine
perfectly manicured nails
of the social worker

crocheting
a pocket full of poems
peaceful thoughts

economic downturn
the boutique owner's
mended blouse

knitting
in the holes of the sweater
ocean sound

snow days
mom lets me watch TV
soap operas

radio off
the night plays on
wind chimes

play
a doll brings
to an empty space
a little heart

angels
the snow accepts the pattern
of our wings

arms wide
even a doll asks
for love

a senior moment
the forgotten haiku
not in the doll

building a snowman
the kid insists on a twig
punk hair style

domino loser
puts another log
on the fires

guidebook
warm in my hands
January beaches

grandchildren gone
she still has glitter on her
cheek
from the card

like all women
wanting to be admired
the doll

old-fashioned
tonight the newest doll
sits on my knee

some people
never grow up
dolls

the tally lengthens
another candlelit evening
of dominoes

the warmth
skating in central park
with jazz

winter leaving
by the beached kayak
patches of snow

winter nights
I only lay the cards out
for solitaire

without blinking
staring at the sunset
dolls in the window

poetry reading
all the folks
in New Orleans
neighbors

blue eyes
above the poetry
FOOF logo

cloak room
among lost coats
a bib

drunk
the poet reads a poem
by someone else

gripping the neck
of his guitar tighter
poetry worse

high top
black tennis shoes
Point Arena

his beaming face
after reading his poems
a sweaty brow

in new jeans
the old guy and
his big belly

in the corner
at a rural poetry reading
three spears

jazz program
all the listeners
are white

moaning
is it the poetry
or the jazz

Odd Fellows Hall
from red hot jazz
to firetrap

old lady voice
higher than the sax
D.H. Lawrence

our well dry
jazz & poetry changes
the wine

passion
free to all
25 listeners

pelvic thrusts
Mississippi river mud
on their minds

poetry reading
all the women bring
their boobs

room too large
candles flicker in the poetry
of black tablecloths

saxophone
the beginning of headache
squawks

so nervous
poets as non-poets read
non-poems

the contest
a slam jazz & poetry
with over-blown roses

the thirty ideas
of the beat poets
autistic audience

thigh high socks
the poetry reading
with the mayor

undercurrents
beneath the jazz noise
broken poems

power outage
ancestor worship
the morning task
of cleaning lamps

another day
the to-do list
goes to page three

boiled eggs
the grumble of thunder
for breakfast

candlelight bath
the basin in the kitchen
quickly cools

counting the days
on emergency rations
empty water jugs

decision made
not to go to the store
flood-closed road

idle hours
knitted together by white
crocheted potholders

in sunshine
a promise of power
PG & E truck

local news
a friend's house crushed
by a tree

local radio station
no news is good news
for the batteries

midst the storm
the quiet of candle shine
ringing the room

more news
no power forecast
until tomorrow

national news
on the battery radio
our storm

newscast over
the next rain storm arrives
at the door

saving a wash-up
eggs are spooned
out of the shell

storm proof
the haiku written
in the dark

sun through clouds
how can it be
still no power

walking wine
to the downed power line
and the repairmen

relatives
reflecting
grandmother's face
the silver moon

her face as story
ancestors who lived
in sod houses

silence
between family members
frames on portraits

winter rain
grandmother babbles
in her dementia

winter street
bringing to an old woman
a chill wind

religion
an act of faith
in total darkness
striking a match

Compline
the iron bell speaks
the last word

hide-bound
the Old Testament
a sacred cow

offering
in the church
our smells

the point
of saving energy
the altar candle

silence
smoke uncurls itself
from incense

TV evangelist
from his Lazy-boy chair
knows our sins

transportation
entering salt point
the windshield is covered
with white crystals

first winter rain
on the highway boats
headed for dry dock

shaking train
is that white cloud
Fuji-san

traffic halt
the pine tree by the road
grows old

war
a desert storm
circling the country
us as enemy

are enemies
as scared of us
as we are

before this war
standing together
the not-yet dead

evening storm
the news of the war
comes as static

more non-news
about weapons' inspection
I turn off the radio

selling survival
equipment with no guarantee
the undertaker

terrorist warning
US bombers fly overhead
in a far-away country

word games
bad jokes
trying to put the fun
in funeral

begonias
first frost and they'll
be gone

buried
in the burned
urn

can you believe
eve knows the time
of evening

chilled children
how to keep a lid
on invalids

dried up
winds swirl through
Stony Creek

his new Jaguar
her foot smoothes again
the carpeting

honeymooners
wanting to stay forever
in Anchor Bay

how does the ear
in a pear taste
silence

how low can you get
on the way down
to a pillow

if fishy are shy
how much of a bass
is . . .

in a fort
of comforters
warm arms

in the park
the ark
of his bark

it can flow
in every flower
or lower

just a pine tree
but it seems to be waving
on Signal Point

Little River Road
in summer it flows
with tourist cars

mother and daughter
no longer sure of which
is witch

Navarro River
every sentence begins with
Oh look!

over
in the clover
a lover

overwhelmed
yet I sail when able
to the table

seasons change
my honey colored hair
now salt & pepper

tea
a good friend with wit
and teasing

the ear in fear
portal of anxiety
museum silence

the haven
was once heaven
all we have

the little dog
turns into a god
no good

the seasons
in a sea of
suns

tickling my foot
waters in the riffles
of Feather River

title
is that the tit of
titillation

to eaves
near waves
a cave

together
putting the we
in wed

together
the possessive words
genital genitive

TV evangelist
mistake on the monitor
Let us prey

vegetarian
yet whatever I eat
is in d*eat*h

where will the will
in willows form the lea
in leaves

without toil
let us oil our palms
with alms

work

bookshelves
all the spider's work
in her web

no nails
the new-coffin smell
of high-tech glue

shining pine
dovetailing together with
carpenter's hands

typing book reviews
a bug in a hard shell squished
with bare fingers

wind up toys
the wiry peddler seems
easily excited

working day
the carpenter off fishing
a crow steals his lunch

writing

a flurry of rain
the pen begins to write
the audible room

a new language
written in my oldest books
mildew

after the contest
vowing to write more
and better

calligraphy screens
too excited to write
a new poem

depths of cloud
the riddle of a poem
found in the sky

gentle waves
the nouns and verbs
of my grammar

it's snowing
turning my head away
from the computer

leading cranes home
the idle hand takes up a pen
to write a few words

leaving it out
of my journal
forget-me-not

moonset
the days I didn't keep
a journal

morning fog
the dream journal
stays open

nodding off
the pen scribbles over
the page

scroll poems
the emperor's wrist moves
on the wall

snow falling
the long awaited letter
on its way

so proud of my letter
then to find out he
never read it

taking a pee
only 1587607 bytes
downloaded

the haiku muscle
getting up early to watch
the moon set

the whole day
with an unknown weed
journaling

writing again
the gods visit us
as one voice

writing haiku
the slow fall of a comet
into the sun

you haven't written
waves half-a-world away
rush to the shore

writing haiku with song titles
Alice blue gown
button up your overcoat
all the way

an occasional man
among my souvenirs
black and blue

at long last love
before the parade passes by
come fly with me

autumn in New York
are you making any money
without a song

babies on Broadway
bewitched, bothered and
bewildered
blame it on my youth

blues in the night
brother can you spare a dime
(for) black coffee

come rain or come shine
I'll hang my tears out to dry
heather on the hill

cottage for sale
the folks who live on the hill
get out of town

crazy she calls me
every time we say good-bye
fools fall in love

friendship
from this moment on
down with love

from this moment on
try a little tenderness
never swat a fly

home on the range
all I do is dream of you
red, hot and blue

just in time
the masquerade is over
love for sale

Linda
keeping out of mischief now
(the) laziest girl in town

lovely to look at
love turned out the light
long ago and far away

Lulu's back in town
how long's this been going on?
little white lies

mister five by five
the lady's in love with you
more than you know

mister wonderful
I get along without you very
well
white lies

my heart stood still
(on a) quiet night of quiet stars
biding my time

my shining hour
the night we called it a day
the tender trap

night and day
all I do is dream of you
cloudy morning

on a night like this
wrap your troubles in dreams
(and) count your blessings

old devil moon
on such a night as this
somebody loves me

over the rainbow
on the street where you live
fools fall in love

put on a happy face
stars fall on Alabama('s)
street of dreams

somebody loves me
it's the talk of the town
after you're gone

strange fruit
swinging on a star
two sleepy people

the ladies who lunch
leaning on a lamppost
making whoopee

the man I love
let's get away from it all
tonight at eight

windmills of your mind
you are driving me crazy
who can I turn to?

for all we know
it's only a paper moon
you got trouble

WINTER Animals

birds
a hawk soars
its shadow watching
me

barefoot in snow
yet still feeding birds
the saint sculpture

between storms
half of the quail family
comes out to eat

colder now
with one crow
a frozen field

coming to the north
when geese have flown
silence

deep skies
have taken the birds
rest of the sun

ducks
floating on the pond
the moon's chill

frost
on the duck's feather
patterns

grace
melting ice on dark water
swans

ground fog
above the pond
snowy egrets

late snow storm
on budded branches piles
of fluffed up birds

low day moon
a crow flies over it with
an alarm squawk

lunch time
a chicken vanishes
in the soup

melting snow
with the white disappears
the cardinal

needing a line
for the poem
a crow flies by

one-legged
that gull flies
higher

snow goose
winter comes to the pond
white on white

snowy graves
bird tracks and then
nothing

sparrows
sharing our rice
with each other

the crow
brings to the frozen limb
black cold

wearing feathers
the messenger braves the cold
moonlight owl

white moves the mist
between frozen reeds
a snowy egret

winter garden
yet the crow finds something
to look for

winter sun
drawn to the persimmon
pecked by a crow

writing
on the smooth snow
crane dances

crawling insects
cold enough to freeze
yet a rain puddle shivers
skating water strider

farm animals
cold enough to snow
by the sheep pen piles
of discarded wool

winter rain
the horse's head bowed
straight down

flying insects
tattered wings
waiting for the doctor
a moth

mice
a few large flakes
mouse tracks on the snow
gray in the blue

bitter cold
the mouse in the trap
the only warmth

hailstones
in the attic the patter
of mice

morning peace
on the doorstep the gift
of two dead mice

not able to think
a mouse nibbling
migraine pills

snow falling
between tones of the bell
mice are born

winter boots
a warm home
for a mouse

pets
a square
of winter sun curved
a cat

at the doorway
puss has no piss
falling snow

first light
at the rain speckled window
the sick cat

his beloved pet
stalking my pets
at the feeder

on his muzzle
now on his grave
hoar frost

lost dog
the sign lies in the ditch
next to road kill

pelting rain
the wet cat licks
her fur

silence
carried into the room
by the deaf cat

the nation at war
my neighbor's pit bull
continues to bark

war news
even the cat refuses
to eat dinner

winter solitude
the cat washes again
the tip of her tail

whales
deep breathing
above the sea surface
whale sprout

migrating whales
my packed suitcase
headed south

without wings or legs
on a 10,000 mile journey
whales – thoughts

water animals
a heart beats
in the sea shell
silence

silence
the age of the turtle
in its shell

wild animals
eating moonlight
on the frosted field
deer

hoarding food
even the ground squirrels
know of war

lynx
mother and kitten
linked

first snow
following bear paw prints
Birkenstocks

on the trail
of a rabbit's snow tracks
fox leaps

tracking in snow
bear paw prints followed
by round eyes

wild rain storm
washing the raccoon tracks
off the soup pot

WINTER Plants

buds
after an illness
wobbly steps in a budding
woods are enough

windless thaw
budding plum bright
with silver drops

winter leaves
buds of tightly rolled
silence

without smoke
laughter in the buds
of marijuana

bushes
bamboo leaves
on the porch boards
yamabuki shadow

California weather
under the snowball bush
roses in bloom

hydrangeas
color taken from ink
in a journal

lost in translation
the Japanese love bush
becomes the Judas tree

voices
between the bushes
a rivalry

blossoms
roads closed
because of flooding
the plum blooms

camellia
a camellia
floating in our conversation
unspoken thoughts

after the accident
all the pain in deep red
camellias

curved petals
from the camellia-scented
candle
dripping wax

knocked off by rain
camellias bloom again
in the puddles

my angry friend
tramping down the path
fallen camellias

charcoal
summer burn
snow melts first around
the charcoal

charred trees
the coldness of cars
driving right by

dead leaves
alive again
the dead leaf drips
melting snow

273

as lips
the curled leaf makes
me smile

falling
with the first snow
a faded leaf

first snow
only dried leaves
are white

ink painting
on the porch floor
leaf shadows

who gave them life
these brown leaves that skitter
over the ice

evergreens
a giant bends
above a chain saw
silence

a walk in the woods
saying *Merry Christmas*
to the perfect pine

anxious
the cypress in a night wind
cracks its branches

bent by sea winds
among mountain pines
I stand tall again

bent pines
all these winters they never
shoveled snow

blue frozen
to the pine cone
night

evergreens
even on spider mites
holiday colors

evergreens in snow
before a black woods
cold but warmer

ever faithful
at Gualala Arts Center
groups of redwoods

flickering
in the white pine
snow shadow

pine fire
the smoke rises up
tree-shaped

pruning
the air moves better
with pine scent

redwood fragrance
the art on the wall
raises a notch

shoreline pines
gazing into the wind
I too twist

silver-tipped firs
snow deepening
silence

snowfall
whiter in the presence
of sequoia trees

winter river
in the living room
an evergreen

fruits
hunger moon
apple on the topmost bough
gone

mountain meadow
the taste of berries to be
in the snow

winter blooms
small and bitter
quince

winter solitude
in the taste of tea
quince flowers

winter sun
sucking each wedge
of the tangerine

flowers
crocus in snow
children stick out their tongues
at each other

delphinium
no one writes about
such old flowers

eco-friendly
but still the funeral hurts
with no flowers

gladiolus
happy to have visitors
to the art center

hospital
the roses already wilted
in the fear

nasturtiums
next to poisonous plants
doctor's office

poised as mouths
with a conversation of petals
orchids

white torches
light the garden path
calla lilies

grass
reeds
frozen to the lake
moon shadow

such cold
the sere grass trembles
in the sun

grains
end of winter
just the smell of rice cooking
fills me up

end of winter
cooking the rice with
unknown leaves

leafless trees
a fallen tree
the river returns
to itself

a grove of ancient oaks
a circle of sun warming
silence

as many forms
as the clay pots
tree sacrifice

cold but warmer
evergreens in snow
before a black woods

frost
in the crotch of a tree
beginning of age

fuel for the fire
trees in all their forms
a pyramid

silence
between the growing rings
in wood

silence
under a tree at noon
a small shadow

thawing ice
cracks in black mud
tree roots

shadows
in river ice cracks
winter trees

tree wisdom
in their shapes
old persons

the drape
of water over rock
a crooked tree

moss
green
melting snow
moss

land's end
on the tips of moss
a radiance begins

no hedges
the old cement walls
totally green

raspberries
best of the jam
found behind a tooth
raspberry seed

low winter sun
in the raspberries
red and green

water plants
foggy shoreline
remains the far mountains
with kelp-green trees

NEW YEAR

NEW YEAR Moods

celebration

another day
behind the mirror
a coming forward

blue skies
the universe permits my need
to be here

end of the year
the museum far away
takes all my beads

generations
ringing the bells singing
old songs

my soul bows down
the majesty of the sea
in me

coping

holiday
for this I chose
to exist

daughter-in-law
her birthday gift to me
canned pickles

first the birds go
then snowflakes come back
to my changes

looking for god
I find in myself
god's eyes

moon set
memories of Christmas past
light my way

the sea enters me
outside of my senses
soul

waiting for dawn
I forget how old
I am

death thoughts

a bird's flight
and then I am gone
and forgotten

no holiday
on this I chose
to exit

death
the sea in me
goes home

dew comes and goes
it's hard to believe
I will follow

ebb tide
we thought we had time
but it was gone

I ask the sea
to keep me
under a rock

meals cooked
and the lives I gave
the right to take mine

the fire laid
down in the sea
me

the suicide
even the sea won't keep
beach debris

when I die
it will be
my ocean

fear

alone
in the monastery
the Virgin Mary

fear at Christmas
gifts
am I good enough

I've lost sight
of the slender moon
again that worry

mid-life crisis
70th birthday roses
hang their heads

firsts

first dream
a lack of boundaries with
a locked gate

first earth
obscuring the coffin
a heaviness

first morning
still trying to perfect
last year's poem

frustration

a new day
the same old me
older

a setting moon
and unfulfilled goals
under the tree

Christmas play
the tall girl who plays Joseph
hates little Mary

end of the day
the cushion as lumpy
as I feel

he asks today
is tomorrow your birthday
married 25 years

how easy to hate
the man who gives
no gifts

how to focus
on the silent breath
one coughing

recycling
her Christmas card
from me last year

sleepy
the rest of the year
has got to be better

the next day
all of my muscles
still sitting

up too early
me and other children
on Christmas morning

gratitude
gifts under the tree
the way babies come
into our lives

gratitude
my head bows more easily
each passing day

kindness and love
with the wrapped gifts
the misty moon

rich housewives
sitting on their cushions
silent snobbishness

short as a child is
I was wiser then and closer
to heaven

spaced out
I forget to pay *dana*
to the guru

joy
Christmas joy
the moon comes closer
full and clear

Christmas play
one wise man prefers to sit
on momma's lap

Christmas tree
lopsided and straggly
how it delights me

coming closer
a perfectly round moon
sometimes I get it right

if I were not here
still between the notes
flute music

my happiness
on the meditation cushion
again

opening gifts
the eagerness for
a New Year

the grief
of being born I've lived
it up in joy

the psalms my palms
I've forgotten how lovely
we all are

the ugly child
finding out at seventy
she was beautiful

under the tree
the quietness of gifts
still wrapped

without a tongue
even fish worms wiggle
speak of joy

offerings
made with tears
watered with a life
offerings – ourselves

oneness
bowing to Buddha
and the day's Indian guru
statue Mary prays

one candle lit
in the Catholic church
a statue of Buddha

one tone
in the shakuhachi
just breath

the world
sitting on my cushion
waves as breath

the zendo
built by Catholics
for rent

your spring rain
entering my autumn leaves
our one world

one year older
breathing
my numbers turn
to years

daydream
getting older it is
a nightmare

waiting
only to realize I am
growing old

younger
by the hours on a beach
the old woman

peace
a million protesters
multiplied by a silence
become the majority

back from the temple
stretched out on the floor
how peaceful you are

patriots for peace
within our land grows
another country

peace on earth
watching the full moon
alone

protest posters
the art – the heart
lacking in Washington

seeking peace
in a noisy household
the world

the kiss of peace
Brother Bell-Ringer avoids
me now

the bell voices
out of our stillness
a wish for peace

questions
can it get better
piles of gifts under
moon radiance

does it ever sleep
the one in me who rows
this empty boat

morning fog
where are all the people
who hurt me

resolutions
a vow of silence
yet in my ears ringing
of the past

determined to
withdraw from the world
falling down flat

New Year's diet
trying to sleep
as late as I can

resolutions
the champagne tastes flat
without bubbles

skipping breakfast
the new year begins
resolute

satisfaction
everything I want
before opening gifts
I have

sadness
drifting fog
it passes so quickly
this life

mourning mothers
faces masked with grief
over ragged children

slipping by
the full moon
my many years

the brother's farewell
so few hours together
so many tears

wishes
January snow
wishing the holiday stuff
was still up

pealing of a bell
deeper into time
the wish for peace

NEW YEAR Occasions

birthdays

between showers
hours come to my birthday
as sunshine

birthday happiness
I complete another trip
around the sun

for my birthday
the sun and the moon
for 24 hours

late evening
light coming from laughter
her birthday

my age
spoken four years ago
a younger sound

new calendar
all of our birthdays
already here

post-birthday blues
one day older and now
it rains

so many gifts
so much light
mine

your birthday
the kind of day
that opens flowers

Christmas

Christmas lights
early in the morning
a full moon

Christmas party
the way to the city blocked
by flooding

coming ashore
on Christmas Day
pure white waves

Merry Christmas
the surf echoes
with a roar

morning light
the world comes together
as Christmas

moon glow
under the Christmas tree
piled packages

on the silver path
of a winter moon
Christmas coming

time to burn
the whole candle
Christmas

under the tree
the final gift of Christmas
the full moon

end of the year

end of the year
a voice tells of the death
of an old friend

heavy rain
the year runs down
to its end

holiday candles
burning down to the end
of the year

open mouths
in the clanging bells
end of a year

New Year's Day

a new year
already the first mistake
1/1/01

end of the first day
fireplace embers burst
into flame

the year begins
on fresh sheets with a new
blanket of snow

New Year's Day
a wind-blown twig
writing on snow

New Year's Day
religious fasting
or the flu

New Year's Day
the amaryllis sprout
appears full

New Year's Day
the tossed coins
fall apart - #23

New Year's morning
yesterday's hot idea
takes all day

snow white birds
on sea-foam beaches
New Year's Day

the ox brings
blossoms from the sun
a new year

New Year's Eve

Happy New Year
in the wood kiln's fire
clay cups' glow

New Year's Eve
still wearing party hats
the old couple

New Year's noise
the map of Japan unfolds
so much unknown

New Year's Party
the future is rosy for everyone
except the lobster

two hands at midnight
on my Mickey Mouse watch
year of the rat

while making tea
I warm milk for the cat
New Year's Eve

Solstice
in the full moon
the spirit of giving
at Winter Solstice

solstice moon
even an old heart
celebrates

solstice sun
standing still at high noon
deep meditation

NEW YEAR Celestial

angels
a cup of spirits
in the wood kiln's fire
midnight glow

in silence
all those no longer here
gather around

silent prayer
lifted up by bells
angels on high

air
white smoke
rising straight into the air
the taken prayer

clouds
another country
the full moon goes into
clouds over the sea

cloud catcher
atop the ridge
a cross

depths of cloud
the riddle of a poem
found in a sky

people for peace
clouds gather from the sea
rise up high

darkness
how the bell speaks
joy in the darkest hour
Blessed Be Blessed

fog
foggy morning
the Christmas gift
wrapped in tissue

missing mass
daybreak in the canyon
filled with fog

heat
woodstove shimmer
the Holy Mother statue
is alive

moon
28 beads
of the moon month
saying the rosary

adding
to the piles of poems
a lone moon

all night
my prayers for peace
the full moon

almost holy
other lives on the moon
craters

anchoring the light
I let the moon slip
into the sea

as a holiday
the moon comes to us
in the far north

Christmas Eve
the full moon low
to light the tree

Christmas moon
even an old heart
celebrates

Christmas morn
moon shine sparkling
on every branch

Christmas tree glow
in a sea of abundance
the full moon

clouded moon
under the Christmas tree
wrapped gifts

cloudless
the year begins with
a full moon

cold night
the full moon warmed
by Mars & Saturn

entering
my vow of silence
the moon

full moon light
figurines coming alive
in the crèche

from land to sea
spanning both years
the 16th night moon

holiday season
the moon gives its full light
to the whole earth

in a calm sea
Christmas tree's glow where
the full moon sets

in the shore pine
a golden ornament
the full moon

moon gifts
under the Christmas tree
wrapped packages

morning light
comes earlier now
a clear full moon

on my rosary
the biggest bead
the moon

my Christmas gift
coming one day early
the full moon

Queen of Heaven
and faith of our fathers
a single moon

solstice moon
the southern most sun
is right here

the gift exchange
radiance of the moon
and a still sea

the moon
beginning the holidays
round – golden

the moon
coming ever closer
to hear the prayers

the moon's silver path
points far to the north
Christmas is coming

moon set
from branch to branch
the setting moon decorates
a shore pine

moonset
memories of Christmas past
light my way

the setting moon
not alone for Christmas
three bright stars

winter radiance
even clouds can't cover
the setting moon

rain
a rain storm
for St. Francis of Assisi day
right out of Italy

first raindrops
the wayward path
of a skipped stone

New Year's Eve
shining in the windows
rain

rainbow
my ancestors
in the rainbow
blessing

prayers for peace
around the dark ocean
a rainbow

sky
Christmas skies
the round heart
of the moon

clear blue
another way comes in
the new year

out of darkness
the countenance of god
morning skies

since today
birds soar through you
the greater sky

sky spirits
dome high to hold
happiness – gratitude

snow

in a white robe
to greet the new year
snowy landscape

joining
my vow of silence
the first snow

stars

another star
has gone home
breath still

mountains
beyond the monastery gate
galaxies

stars shining
in the ridge-top pine
Christmas

stars twinkle
in time with their pulse
voices chanting

storm

all gifts opened
the tree lights have gone out
in the storm

storm-churned
the moon serenely sets
in the sea

storm warnings
the year is about
to its end

sun

after the storm
drops of sunshine
as decorations

in gratitude
the hours come to my birthday
as sunshine

birthday happiness
I complete another trip
around the sun

Christmas over
the sun returns
for spring

day after Christmas
gliding over the sea
a new sun

faith in the fog
I salute the setting sun
and rising moon

first dream
after a week of rain
sunshine

gateway to the night
an altar candle replaces
the sun

sitting *zazen*
with me the sun
comes and goes

storm of the century
snow darkens the capital
protesters in sunshine

sun and moon
in one morning
a complete birthday

today is the day
the South's great dance of fire
invited – celebrated

sunrise
at the monastery
the strange sexual weather
of sunrise

lauds
before sunrise
our praising

singing
up the sunrise
desert monks

sunrise sunset
the glorious times
closed in chapel

sunrise
the moon's glow
before it sets

sunset
end of the light
for the day or a life
only poems left

thunder and lightning
loud and clear
thunder and lightning
the word of god

winds
silent prayer
and then the wind
begins to blow

streaming hair
spirits of the east called
for gentle winds

sun shine
wind blows away
another year

NEW YEAR Terrestrial

beach
how easy to kneel
at the altar of a beach
holy ground

voices mingling
in the roar of the surf
Happy New Year

canyon
canyon chapel
the voice of god
in stone walls

on two sides
the word of god
canyon walls

red white and black
the monks move among
the canyon walls

desert
monks' voices
deep in the desert
keeping it alive

earth
spirits of earth
in this tree box find
your children

hills
vespers
on the high hill
me and a cloud

rivers
a flowing brook
the pope's funeral ends
in a flood of tears

a new year
yet rain falls down
and rivers rise

lying in the stream
at first it clouds and then
I am clear

on New Year's Day
our rivers runneth over
all roads closed

the evergreen
in the living room
winter river

the old koan
what was I before I was born
naked in a summer river

rocks
all around our
millennium celebration
million-year old rocks

a voice
with the word of god
river stones

creeks of gray rock
sunset's flash of cinnabar
liquefies the air

moving stones
in the shrine river
women dancing

seas
across the sea
on the moon's silver path
Christmas is coming

breaking waves
the moon's silver path
heals the water

in a rippled sea
Christmas tree's glow
the full moon sets

living by the sea
I cannot grow old or
wish for paradise

never older
the ocean sings to you
Happy Birthday

the day I die
I will enter the sea
without drowning

thunder
in the New Year
huge waves

NEW YEAR Livelihood

adornment
new perfume
a someone else
is me

candles and lighting
a misty moon
sets between them
holiday candles

as candle glow
the setting moon
is warming

candlelight
it slowly finds the faces
radiant with joy

candle shadows
the night gives up
the shape of things

holiday candles
a misty moon sets between
stars

holiday candles
light to the end
of the year

lighting a candle
the room seems warmer
above the gifts

off the grid
the plea of an altar candle
for a short night

reflected fire
the setting moon touches
the unlit candle

smoke
incense unrolls
itself

with the smell
of candle wax
mass ends

cleaning and recycling
filling the drawer
the old calendar
all of its days

fresh and clean
the pillowcase too forgot
last night's dream

freshly clean
to greet the new year
soapsuds and snow

housecleaning
and yet the mountains
are cloud-swept

in a white robe
to greet the new year
smell of soap

new calendar
hanging it higher
to hide a stain

tree down
in the bare clean house
the body removed

concerts

bells and flute go
Tell it on the Mountain
benediction

bells
lifting to heaven
our eyes

bells ringing
high and low
tap of feet

mic hum
the flute master appreciates
the company

late evening
light coming from the drum
as the sound of bells

death and funerals

anchored by rocks
shadows of the spirit ship
aground

at the funeral
between prayers
a ticking clock

cradled rocks
in the spirit ship
some body

floating
above the spirit ship
a rocky cliff

flung rocks
lying in the spirit ship
someone's body

shadow shape
the spirit boat goes
into light

spirit ship
only a shadow of itself
goes aground

education

grand master
passing on the tradition
breathing

teaching us
the guru rubs his toes
as he sniffs

walking meditation
the guru breaks the silence
with the smell of his feet

foods and feeding

a cup of tea
touch of a potter's hand
in winter cold

after dinner
fear and loathing
a belch

a vegetarian
with legs crossed in *zazen*
the roasting chicken

backwoods new year
gunshots from the neighbor
with an illegal deer

bean soup
noise lost in the noise
of the new year

church bells
the butcher who cheats
stops to pray

drinking tea
the silence warms
the slurp

promises
unpacking the candy molds
on New Year's Day

such a man you are
under pure white frosting
chocolate cake

the Christmas fire
with cake and wine
fruitwood

heating
layer on layer
clay and wood fuel
prayers

logs ablaze
saying *Happy New Year*
our lips touch

New Year's Day
the warmth of touching
dulcimer strings

holidays and customs
already enough
unopened presents
and a full moon

Christmas bazaar
the carefully tied bow
crooked

Christmas Eve
the talk show theme
teen-age pregnancy

Christmas lights
two cop cars stop
the drunk

Christmas music
on the freeway red lights
cars stopping

Christmas play
the giant leap from Jesus
to Santa Claus

Christmas quiet
all those no longer here
gather around

cloud covered moon
my eyes turn back
to the lighted tree

clouded moon
under the Christmas tree
wrapped gifts

from living with us
the holiday greens turned
to gold

frosted glass
birthday candles warm
mild jokes

more eggnog
figures coming alive
in the crèche

gifts
the wound that protects
a secret

in a north window
reflecting Christmas lights
the setting moon

in the yard
six junked cars and plastic
Christmas decorations

New Year's Day
good wishes sent out
return tenfold

on my Christmas list
from over the dark hill
the full moon

opening gifts
taking the bandage
off the wound

opening gifts
the tree light go out
in the splendor

new year's noisemakers
by the bed one shoe drops
and then the other

remote sea coast
no Christmas lights in sight
to mar the beauty

scattered toys
under the tree
pine cones

sea-still world
Christmas comes only
when the tree is lit

stamps
giving away the secret
of gifts under the tree

the gift exchange
radiance of the full moon
and a still sea

the neighbor
with the most lights
not paying his bills

tied to nature
a sprig of evergreen
pinned to my shirt

red-nosed in the fog
Rudolph the reindeer
as lawn decoration

throwing beans
throwing out the devil
my neighbor

under the tree
the final gift of Christmas
the setting moon

houses and home
Christmas decorations
even the smallest house has
a wreath of smoke

my room so small
the moon appears at once
in both windows

new calendar
the days of meaning
wait to be marked

strange on our street
the junky cars of rich kids
home for the holidays

religion
after Compline
in the nightly silence
snoring

all male
monastery rules
the Virgin Mary

alone
with god the Protestant's
wobbly bow

a monk taps
the wooden bell
the rain stops

ancestors
who have fired pots like this
teach me more

a photo
of the Zen Master
empty frame

a small box
all the way from India
the Buddha's smile

a vow of silence
trying quietly to leave
a fart

breaking
my vow of silence
chapel bells

buying a Buddha
only later remembering
I'm a Methodist

celibate
yet a billion people call him
Holy Father

celibate monks
the question of eternal life
comes to an end

cold morning
the moon and I together
saying the rosary

collection plate
altar lilies bend to give
golden pollen

cooling breeze
the temple flag is
unmoved

coming to the temple
tea and haiku parties
moonlight

desert prayer
of folded hands
holding a house

evening prayers
the shape of flame
on the cooled pot

fog
touching myself
prayer

from the west
the element of water protects
the fire from us

frost shimmers
from the temple roof
prayers ascend

golden Buddha
discovering he's made of straw
inside

good ol' boy
system peaks out
the monastery

incense
coming into the church
Christmas

lights
going to the darkened church
our footsteps

making a church
out of the community center
Christmas carols

matins
in the clean kitchen
me and a mop

mountain masters
with mountain wisdom
a plain girl child

moss on her lips
yet still saying prayers
to the stone goddess

my native land
yet a stranger in a community
of monks

out of darkness
people appear on a path
to the chapel

out of stillness
the sound of peace
bell voices

pilgrim path
to the river god's temple
in a blue haze

prayers begin
with the clanging of the bell
of the buoy

Protestant
communion with cold water
Premium crackers

Quaker meeting
the wood fire speaking
in tongues

raked sand
in the Zen garden
my footprints

released from stone
temple entrance demons
in the storm

religion
on the remote coast
buoy bells

Spirits of Place
hey! join the party
partake of cornmeal

spirits of the north
bring your paint boxes
to manifest colors

still asleep
everyone but the bald monks
praying at dawn

temple
where no women are allowed
many cats

the lone woman
permitted in the monastery
Virgin Mary

the mysteries
move to the altar
bell tones

the narrow path
my two feet walk
religion

the offering
plate fills with cash
ringing bells

voice of a bell
bringing out the joy
of hope and peace

weathered wood
yet on the Buddha's chest
traces of gold

with no music
we call in the spirits
by clapping hands

without words
a hand on the knee
god is there

writing

in a book
looking up the moon
it's gone

the shape of poems
when light shines through
sounds

hands folded
unable to write
in prayer

thunderheads
coming together at the sea
haiku retreat

NEW YEAR Animals

birds

a bird soars
where the sky is clear
you already are
- for Davina Kosh

birds fly up
in the face of the unknown
prayers

Christmas cookies
in the sea gull's beak
a starfish

holy white
from wave to wave
the gull

many pigeons
the compassion goddess
in her temple

new job
the crane lifts its foot
for a first step

New Year's Day
a towhee turning over one leaf
then another

New Year's morning
a stunned sparrow staggers
on the porch

peaceful nature
the crow-hawk fight
in my meditation

pigeons flying
the names of saints chanted
by a lone man

Sunday church
on the sunny porch
me and a sparrow

cats

birthday gift
the outdoor cat brings me
a wood tick

early to bed
the cat that bothers
the Christmas tree

fresh flowers
before the unknown shrine
two motley cats

New Year's Day 2003
the cat retracts his claws
during the news cast

new year's party
only the cat stays awake
until midnight

purring peace
the setting moon brings
a cat to my lap

the year ends
in a dry green tree
the kitten

dogs
pooches for peace
at a demonstration on Market
Street
a fight breaks out

walking meditation
my neighbor unleashes his
dog
and smiles

insects
buzzing
only the flies have no
vow of silence

end of the millennium
time and time again
crickets in the night

house rules
spiders have rights too
live and let live

into the cracks
goes prayers for forgiveness
out comes a spider

not keeping
my vow of silence
chapel cricket

offered to the gods
ants and bees accept
the gift of rice

walking
meditation with my partner
the spider

wall decoration
a wooden crucifix
and flies

whales
holiday joy
the sea is full
of whales

all wishes filled
the New Year's sea
full of whales

wild animals
gray robed monk
nibbling grass at the
monastery
a rabbit

rain storm
yet the raccoon comes for
holiday leftovers

NEW YEAR Plants

bulbs
in the window
the amaryllis bulb
pine candles

new sprout
the amaryllis reaches
New Year's Day

new sprouts
after the second storm
around the crocus

flowers
a plant saint
making the world purer
the lily

birthday surprise
the flowers she sent
match his eyes

holy pagoda
the first day
of the rosebud

Indian drum songs
the Christmas cactus
drops a flower

Lotus-Born One
reincarnation repeats
in petals' white

new years
bringing peach blossoms
to flower shops

your birthday
the kind of day
that opens flowers

leaves
deformed in death
yellow print on ice
of a maple hand

pines
bringing in the tree with
spiders and dropped needles
how clean the room smells

Christmas
giving the pine tree
its smell

Christmas lights
in the thick pine forest
a rising moon

decorating
the crooked shore pine
Christmas morn

ending the year
glint of candle light
on pine needles

going to church
in the huge windows
very old pines

no stars
for the crooked shore pine
moonset ornaments

piñon fragrance
my rustic room filled
with the Holy Ghost

snow-melt
the Christmas tree
still brown

sparkling branches
of the crooked shore pine
a hidden moon

winter solstice
lighting up dark houses
evergreen trees

trees
fingers
touching the trees
the flute

the full moon sinks
into my neighbor's trees
Christmas

snowfall
holier in the presence
of tall trees

the darkened tree
with points of light
far out at sea

tree lights
early in the morning
a full moon

trees as trees
the dawn light reveals
the nature of ghosts

wind in trees
listening to music
never heard before

wood to wood
the flute brings the trees
into swaying

vegetables
was it once
such a white cloud
the cauliflower

weeds
Zen gardening
the weed breaks off
to leave its root

Jane Reichhold was born as Janet Styer in 1937 in Lima, Ohio, USA. She has had over forty books of her haiku, renga, tanka, and translations published. Her latest book by Kodansha USA, is *Basho The Complete Haiku*. As founder and editor of AHA Books, Jane has also published *Mirrors: International Haiku Forum, Geppo,* for the Yuki Teikei Haiku Society, and she has co-edited with Werner Reichhold, *Lynx* for Linking Poets since 1992. *Lynx* went online in 2000 in AHApoetry.com the web site Jane started in 1995. Since 2006 she maintains an online forum – AHAforum. She lives near Gualala, California with Werner, her husband, and a Bengal cat named Buddha.

Jane was a twice winner of the Museum of Haiku Literature Award [Tokyo]. Three-time winner of a Haiku Society of America Merit Book Award: *Tigers In A Tea Cup, Silence,* and *A Dictionary of Haiku (first edition).* Winner of numerous haiku awards, including second place in the 1987 Japan Air Lines contest and in the Itoen Tea Company Award in 1992.

Books

Shadows on an Open Window, Humidity Productions: 1979.
Installation: Collage in Space, Humidity Productions: 1982.
From the Dipper...Drops, Humidity Productions: 1983.
Duet for One Mirror, Humidity Productions: 1984.
Thumbtacks on a Calendar, Humidity Productions: 1985.
Reissnaegal auf einem Kalender, 1985, (Translation of *Thumbtacks* in German).
Cherries/Apples, Humidity Productions: 1986.
Graffiti, Humidity Productions: 1986.
As Stones Cry Out, Humidity Productions: 1987.
Tigers in a Tea Cup, AHA Books: 1988. Haiku Society Merit Book Award
The Land of Seven Realms, Edited. AHA Books: 1988.
A Literary Curiosity: Pyramid Renga "Open," with Bambi Walker, AHA Books: 1989.
Narrow Road to Renga, AHA Books: 1989.
A Gift of Tanka, AHA Books: 1990.
Those Women Writing Haiku. AHA Online Book: 1990 - 2001
Round Renga Round, Edited AHA Books: 1990.
silence, AHA Books: 1991. Haiku Society of America Merit Book Award.
A Dictionary of Haiku, AHA Books: 1992.
Trashopper Haique, AHA Books: 1992.
Classical Mega-Brain Potential, AHA Books: 1992.
Inksmith, with Werner Reichhold. AHA Books: 1992.
Wave of Mouth Stories, AHA Books: 1993.

A Dictionary of Haiku as Four Seasons, bilingual English–Chinese. Yilin Press, Nanking: 1991.
Oracle, with Werner Reichhold. AHA Books: 1993.
Wind Five Folded, Edited with Werner Reichhold. AHA Books: 1992
Bowls I Buy, AHA Online Book: 1996.
Banana Skies – A Play. AHA Online Book: 1997.
Giants' Highway. AHA Online Book: 1993.
In the Presence, with Werner Reichhold, AHA Books: 1997.
Invitation, with Werner Reichhold. AHA Books: 1998.
Geography Lens, AHA Books: 1999.
Her Alone AHA Online Book: 2001.
Journal Journeys. AHA Online Book: 2002.
Writing and Enjoying Haiku: A Hands-On Guide, Kodansha: 2003.
Ten Years Haikujane, AHA Books: 2008.
Basho's Complete Haiku, Kodansha: 2008.
A Tear Out of Renga with Marlene Mountain, AHA Online Book, 2008.
Tanka Splendor, Editor, AHA Books Online: 2002, 2003, 2004, 2005, 2006, 2007, 2008.
Twenty Years of Renga: The Participation Renga from Lynx 1987 - 2007. Jane and Werner Reichhold, editors. AHA Books Online: 2007
Twenty Years Tanka Splendor, AHA Books, Editor: 2009.
Scarlet Scissors Fire. Jane Reichhold. AHA Books: 2009.
Circus Forever. Jane Reichhold with Peter Goetsche. AHA Books: 2010
A Film of Words with Werner Reichhold. AHA Book: 2010.
AHA The Anthology, editor, AHA Books: 2012.
Naked Rock, AHA Books: 2013.
      (Online books can be seen at AHApoetry.com/onlinbk2.htm)

Books of Translation

White Letter Poems by Saito Fumi, AHA Books: 1998.
Heavenly Maiden Tanka by Akiko Baba, AHA Books: 1999.
A String of Flowers, Untied. . . Love Poems from Tale of Genji by Murasaki Shikibu, Stone Bridge Press: 2002.
Breasts of Snow: The Life and Tanka of Fumiko Nakajo, The Japan Times: 2004.
Taking Tanka Home, AHA Books. First Edition: 2010; Second Edition with Aya Yuhki: 2011.

Made in the USA
San Bernardino, CA
04 September 2016